THE SOVEREIGN SELF

Emotional Mastery for
Women in Their Sixties
and Beyond

STACEY DUTTON

Zen on the Hill
NEW MILFORD, CONNECTICUT

Zen on the Hill/Stacey Dutton
New Milford, Connecticut
Website: LiveSovereignSelf.com
Email: stacey@livesovereignself.com

Cover design by Gus Yoo
Editing and book production by Stephanie Gunning

The Sovereign Self/Stacey Dutton—1st edition

Library of Congress Control Number: 2025921058

ISBN 979-8-9931397-0-8 (paperback)
ISBN 979-8-9931397-2-2 (epub ebook)

To my mother, who did not live to see sixty, and whose absence shaped me as much as her presence did.

CONTENTS

The Life That Brought Me Here

I was born into a life already shaped by loss. When my mother was seven months pregnant with me and raising my older sister, my father died suddenly of a brain aneurysm. She was left to navigate young motherhood and sudden widowhood at the same time—grieving and caretaking in the same breath. That early complexity imprinted something deep in me: the understanding that life can be both beautiful and brutal, and that endurance often begins long before we understand what we're carrying.

By the time I was nine, my mother had remarried, given birth to my younger sister, and was diagnosed with breast cancer. I remember the atmosphere of our home shifting with her diagnosis; it suddenly seemed darker and more fragile. Illness and uncertainty became my familiar companions. I learned early that stability is not promised, and that strength often arrives in unglamorous forms.

At fifteen, I went away to boarding school. After graduation, I moved to New York City to attend college and begin shaping a life that was fast, full, and creatively charged.

Subsequently, I worked in the music industry, married at twenty-seven, and became a mother to two children. When they were still very small, my marriage ended. I navigated single motherhood during some of the most demanding years of my life. At forty, I transitioned into television and became the host of one of the earliest home design shows on TLC, *Clean Sweep*. At forty-two, I got remarried. By then, I had learned how to rebuild a life on my own terms.

What followed was a vibrant stretch of years as a casting director, producer, and creator in the reality television genre. I loved the work—the pace, the creative challenge, the way stories were shaped in real time. But in my mid-fifties, the industry began to slow its response. The energy shifted. And slowly, I felt myself aging out of the story the industry wanted to tell.

The COVID pandemic arrived just as I was approaching my sixties, casting a stark, unfamiliar stillness over a life that had always moved at full speed. It marked a liminal threshold—not just for the world, but for me personally—a moment when time slowed enough to make visible what had long gone unattended. And with it, a near-total pause. Work fell away. The structures I had built my life around no longer held. My children were grown. My body—never passive—began to assert itself through broken bones, autoimmune disruptions, and new limitations. I felt a persistent sadness that wasn't attached to an event like a loss or a trauma. Underneath everything, a persistent, quietly disorienting series of questions emerged.

_ Who am I now?

_ What is my value now that I'm no longer working at the same pace?

_ What is my purpose when I'm no longer needed in the same ways?

_ What do I do with the grief I am feeling that has no specific name—only a shape, a weight?

There were no easy answers to these questions. What came instead was a deepening of my sorrow, which had become a full-fledged depression. Sometimes grief lingers, deepens and entangles with other unresolved pain (trauma, isolation, absence of support) until it begins to take on the shape of depression. It's a shifting of the emotional current from sorrow to stagnation, from mourning what was lost to losing sight of oneself.

In my case, there were long walks in the woods. Silence. Stillness. Meditation. Lots of reading. Therapy. And eventually, a kind of homecoming—not to the woman I had been, but to the one I have always been and had nearly forgotten. The one who has existed beneath every role I've played, every achievement, every reinvention.

This book was born from that return. It's written for every woman in her sixties who is moving through uncertainty, through change, through the reckoning that so often arrives in this chapter of life. It's for the woman approaching her sixtieth birthday who's wondering what lies ahead of her and how to live well going forward. It's for the woman who feels unmoored at this stage of her life, who is grieving something she cannot quite name, who is asking deeper questions, such as *Is this all there is? And if not, what comes next?*

If you are wrestling with the same questions or feelings, or musing about your identity in this next stage of your life, please know that you are not broken. You are not behind. You are not done. You are still becoming. And there is power, beauty, and extraordinary hope in that becoming.

My "wrestling" with my questions and feelings is how I got to the place where I am today: deep in the midst of living the return to the me who is behind every role I've ever played.

My hope is that these pages will offer you not only perspective, but also permission. To slow down. (But only if you want to.) To deepen. To let go. To begin again. To live your life not as a reaction, but as a sovereign expression of who you truly are.

The Alchemy of Emotional Mastery

By the time we reach our sixties we have lived a multitude of lives within a single lifetime. We have borne witness to history, to heartbreak, to the revolutions of the self. We've inhabited roles as daughters, lovers, mothers, professionals, creators, and caretakers, and now, we have become something altogether different: a woman untethered from expectation, standing at the threshold of her own uncharted terrain.

And yet, despite our vast experience, the emotional landscapes of our current or impending decade present a different kind of reckoning to us. The external architecture of our lives may be quieter—with children grown and careers shifting or, in some cases, concluded—but the internal terrain is anything but quiet.

Here, in the liminal space between what was and what remains, we are confronted with a choice of whether to resist change, by clinging to old frameworks of identity, or to engage in a deeper, more radical activity—the mastery of the self.

The Sovereign Self is not a book of platitudes. It is also not a guide to "embracing aging" in the reductive, saccharine way our culture often prescribes for aging women, whom it often seems like it would love to stick on a shelf and forget. Instead, it is an exploration of what it means to be truly emotionally agile in our sixties—not simply resilient in the face of loss, but expansive in the face of possibility—and enjoying ourselves as best we can.

We are no longer striving. We are refining.

And therein lies our power.

In *The Sovereign Self,* I am attempting to guide you through consideration of some key themes that typically arise in women's lives in their sixties, themes that are often aspects of the emergence of new identities. Little of the change you can expect to experience is sudden, but it can be helpful to go into it with your eyes wide open. This decade is your time. Your life. Your chance for new measures of freedom.

The book unfolds in three movements: the first explores the inner landscape of reckoning and renewal; the second turns toward the practices and shifts that cultivate sovereignty in daily life; and the third lifts our gaze outward to the freedom, creativity, and legacy that become possible when we inhabit this stage fully. These parts are not as much prescriptions as invitations for you to deepen, to expand, and to become more yourself than you may ever have been before.

PART ONE

FOUNDATIONS OF INNER POWER

ONE

The Architecture of Emotional Mastery

"You have power over your mind—not outside events. Realize this, and you will find strength."

MARCUS AURELIUS

For a woman to be emotionally masterful in her sixties is not about mere resilience; it is about refinement. It is not about enduring hardship, but about engaging with life's complexities with intention, intelligence, and grace.

EMOTIONAL MASTERY AS A DISCIPLINE

By our stage of life, we have encountered loss, reinvention, and profound shifts in identity. We have known both the exhilaration of new beginnings and the ache of things left behind. And yet, despite all we have lived through, true emotional mastery is not something we inherit simply because of experience. Rather, it is something we cultivate with discipline.

The difference between women who struggle through their later years and those who move through them with deep, unshakable presence is not related to their circumstances. It depends on their level of emotional mastery. Those who engage with their emotions deliberately, rather than being ruled by them, typically step into a state of emotional sovereignty—a place where external forces no longer dictate their internal stability.

MASTERY VS. SOVEREIGNTY

Mastery, in its truest sense, is about deep under-standing more than control. To master our emotions does not mean suppressing them or forcing ourselves into an artificial state of positivity. It means learning to engage with our emotions as they arise, discerning which of them requires action and which requires release. It means standing in the midst of uncertainty, grief, or change and responding rather than reacting.

Sovereignty is the natural result of emotional mastery. When a woman reaches a place where her emotions no longer control her—a place where she can sit with discomfort without fear or experience joy without guilt—she becomes sovereign over her inner world. She is no longer subject either to the whims of others or to old wounds and the weight of societal expectations. She does not seek permission to feel, to express, or to change. She moves through life with an authority that cannot be given or taken away.

4

If emotional mastery is the discipline, emotional sovereignty is the reward.

THE MIND AS AN EMOTIONAL ATHLETE

Much like physical strength, emotional mastery requires active engagement. A woman does not wake up one morning emotionally agile, just as she does not develop high muscle tone overnight. Emotional engagement is a practice, like going to Pilates class or lifting weights a few times a week. And yet, many women enter their sixties believing that emotional maturity should be automatic, a natural byproduct of their age.

This is a fallacy. A woman who neglects her emotional strength and agility will find herself bound by old wounds, reactive tendencies, and outdated narratives.

But a woman who deliberately trains her mind—who practices stillness, discernment, and inquiry—will discover a different reality. She will no longer be pulled into every emotional undercurrent. She will not be at the mercy of her past. She will move through her days with a kind of cultivated stillness, unshaken by the temporary and attuned to what truly matters.

This is the foundation of everything that follows in her life.

MOVING FROM REACTION TO RESPONSE

Most of us have spent decades refining our intellects, our careers, and our relationships. But how much time have we truly dedicated to refining our emotional responses? How often have we paused before reacting, not to suppress an arising emotion, but so we could fully understand it?

Have you?

The shift from reaction to response is one of the defining markers of emotional mastery.

It indicates that we have the ability to experience an emotion without becoming consumed by it. It means we are capable of recognizing anger without lashing out, feeling sadness without spiraling into despair, and acknowledging uncertainty without letting it erode our confidence.

Reaction is instinctual, whereas response is intentional. Reaction is dictated by past conditioning. Response is shaped by present awareness. Reaction is what happens when we let emotions drive us. Response is what happens when we sit in the seat of our own sovereignty.

THE TYRANNY OF PAST PATTERNS

By the time we reach our sixties, we have accumulated decades of emotional conditioning. The ways we respond to conflict, disappointment, and change are often echoes of responses learned long ago—some inherited from family, some shaped by culture, some simply habitual. And for many of us, our emotional patterns from earlier in life remain entrenched.

These patterns include:

⟲ The need to please, to keep the peace, to smooth over tension.

⟲ The impulse to withdraw or become small when faced with confrontation.

⟲ The reflex to overextend, to fix, to take responsibility for others' emotions.

⟲ The belief that emotions should be either hidden or justified.

These patterns are not random flaws. At one time, they were survival strategies, which may have been successful in protecting us and helping us get our needs met. But in this stage of life, they are no longer necessary. In fact, they are barriers to our expressions of our sovereignty and keep us tethered, internally, to old versions of ourselves instead of allowing us to fully inhabit the women we have become.

Mastery begins when we can look at our patterns with curiosity instead of judgment.

MASTERING THE PAUSE

The simplest and most profound practice of emotional mastery is the *pause:* the space between feeling and acting.

When an emotion arises, before speaking, before making a decision, before letting the feeling dictate the moment, pause. Observe the sensation, name it, and ask yourself:

- *What is this emotion trying to tell me?*
- *Is this a present response, or an old wound resurfacing?*
- *Do I need to act, or do I simply need to feel?*

The woman who masters the pause masters herself. She moves through life deliberately, intentionally. She is the architect of her emotions. And in designing her responses to people and events, she steps fully into the realm of emotional sovereignty, a space where she is no longer controlled by fleeting emotions, but instead moves through them with wisdom, power, and grace.

DETACHMENT WITHOUT DISCONNECTION

There is a common misconception that emotional mastery requires *detachment:* the ability to remain unaffected, untouched, and above it all. But I would propose that true mastery does not require us to stop feeling our feelings. Mastery is about how well we regulate them. It is about engagement without entanglement. To be sovereign over our emotions does not mean we have the ability to suppress them. It also does not mean we have become indifferent to loss, impervious to criticism, or are untouched by love. It means that we know where we end and the rest of the world begins. It means we can feel deeply without being destabilized.

THE DIFFERENCE BETWEEN ATTACHMENT AND PRESENCE

Many of us have spent much of our lives over identifying with our emotions. A loved one is upset and we feel their pain as if it is our own. A disappointment arises and we internalize it as a failure. We are also conditioned to absorb the emotional currents around us, often without questioning whether they belong to us in the first place.

But attachment to emotion is not the same as presence with emotion. Attachment pulls us into the drama of every passing feeling, making us reactive, defensive, or overwhelmed, whereas presence allows us to acknowledge an emotion, experience it fully, and choose our responses to events (and emotions) from a place of clarity.

To practice detachment without disconnection is to:

◯ Learn the art of witnessing.

9

⤳ Feel sadness without collapsing into it.

⤳ Love deeply without losing yourself.

⤳ Experience disappointment without letting it redefine your worth.

HOLDING SPACE FOR AN EMOTION, NOT BECOMING IT

An emotional master understands that she is the space in which emotions arise and pass. She has learned to grieve without becoming consumed by it, to acknowledge anger without letting it corrode her, and to experience joy without clinging to it in fear of its loss.

The key to emotional sovereignty is to remain fully engaged with life while standing firmly in our own point of view. An emotional sovereign has the ability to witness emotions occurring—both her own and those of others—without losing her balance. The practice of stepping back and witnessing allows life to move through us instead of allowing it to control us.

An emotionally sovereign woman does not retreat from the world. She engages more deeply than most of us—but her engagement takes place on her own terms, in her own time, and from a place of grounded presence, emotional clarity, and hard-won self-knowledge.

THE FOUNDATION OF A SOVEREIGN LIFE

Emotional mastery is neither a concept that we should reserve for spiritual retreats nor is it an abstract theory. It is the groundwork for a life that is sovereign—meaning, one in which our actions are intentional and internally aligned with our values, desires, and purposes. Without aligning ourselves with something we care about, we will be pulled off course by the momentum of external forces—by other people's moods, society's expectations for us, and outdated narratives about who we are that we bought into. With emotional mastery, we can return to ourselves. Again and again.

By our sixties, emotional mastery has become more than useful, it has become essential. Wouldn't you agree? Any new emotional architecture you construct now will determine how you experience not just the current decade, but every year that follows it.

SELF-MASTERY IS NOT ISOLATION

Don't worry. To master your emotional world you do not have to isolate yourself from others. In fact, do the opposite. Open up. Mastery allows us to experience deeper connection with others because it is not built on neediness, performance, or self-abandonment. Remember, you no longer have to mold yourself to fit someone else's comfort. You do not need to explain your emotions to justify their validity. You do not need to fix others in order to feel whole. Far from indifference, this is the boundary that protects both your integrity and theirs.

This is not coldness or detachment.

This is self-possession.

From a centered, self-regulated state of being, you can choose connection—fully, consciously, and without cost to your own integrity.

THE DECADE OF DISCERNMENT

If the earlier decades of your life were marked by ambition, striving, or accumulation, the years that follow will bring you relief. The seventh decade of our lives is a decade of discernment. At sixty, we begin to ask ourselves questions like:

☉ What is essential to me?

☉ What no longer serves me?

☉ Who am I when I am not performing a role?

Emotional mastery will give you the clarity to answer these questions—not as a reaction to fear or loss, but as a movement toward truth. It is the inner scaffolding that allows each mature woman to pare down the noise and build a life that is exquisitely hers.

LIVING AS THE ARCHITECT OF
YOUR EXISTENCE

Most people inhabit their emotional lives the way they would inhabit a house built for them by someone else. They live within the confines of what has been handed to them—beliefs, behaviors, assumptions. But a woman in mastery is the architect of her existence. She chooses what stays and what goes. She redesigns her inner world at her own volition, to match the elegant integrity of who she's becoming. Never for the sake of anyone else's approval.

From a refined, rooted, and sovereign posture, she moves through her life with her head held high, her heart open, and her presence unmistakably her own.

BECOMING THE WOMAN
YOU WERE MEANT TO BE

At this stage of life, the most courageous act may not be reinvention. It may be remembrance. Not becoming someone new, but returning to, and being, the self you've always been beneath the noise, the roles, the expectations.

You're not experiencing a crisis of identity. You are undergoing refinement. Distillation.

A deep homecoming.

The woman who emerges in her sixties is not defined by her past, but informed by it. She no longer needs to prove her worth—she simply lives it. She speaks less to be heard and more to be clear. She shows up not to please, but to be present.

There is a grace in this stage of life. No matter what you've heard, it is not passive. The life of a sixty-something woman is not defined by quiet compliance or gentle retreat. She embodies the grace of discernment, of depth, of unapologetic clarity.

To become the woman you are meant to be is not to strive—it is to shed.

To stop asking for permission.

To stop explaining your choices.

To stop silencing what you know to be true.

This chapter of life does not demand that you start over. It invites you to go deeper.

This is the evolution of identity: not a departure from who you were, but a return to who you are—unmasked, unedited, and entirely sovereign.

REFLECTION AND INTEGRATION

At the end of every chapter in this book you will be offered a few journaling prompts, as invitations for your sovereign self to emerge. In a notebook, write about the following questions.

- *When in my life have I felt most in possession of myself?*

- *What parts of me have been waiting patiently to be reclaimed?*

_ꙅ_ In what ways have I been seeking permission to change?

TWO

The Evolution of Identity

"He who is brave is free."

SENECA

By the time a woman reaches her sixties, she has lived through dozens of incarnations of herself: the daughter, the partner, the mother, the professional, the caretaker, the achiever, the peacemaker. These roles, while meaningful, are often constructed in response to the needs of others—to expectations, to family systems, to social scripts that were never designed with her full humanity in mind. But what happens when those roles begin to dissolve?

SHEDDING THE SKIN OF WHO WE WERE

This is the reckoning of a woman's third act: the realization that the scaffolding of identity built over decades—often unconsciously—no longer holds. The

17

titles she carried no longer define her. And for many a woman, the habits that sustained her now feel like constraints. In their place, a strange and liberating question emerges: *Who am I when I am no longer being the person I've always been?* This questioning of identity does not represent a midlife crisis; nor is it an indicator of a woman's existential unraveling. The inquiry is an invitation to reclaim what was never fully lived. To examine what may have been sacrificed for the sake of survival. It is the beginning of a slow, sacred process of returning to the self—not the self that was shaped for others, but the one that has been waiting to be remembered.

THE INVISIBLE WEIGHT WE CARRY

For many of us, our sixties come with an unexpected emotional weight. Not the heaviness of a dramatic upheaval from loss or trauma, although those experiences may have happened, but from an emotion that's quieter and harder to name. Often, it arrives without a clear trigger. This is a subtle heaviness. A vague sense of being unmoored. Women describe it differently: a loss of energy, a disinterest in things that once mattered, a mild, underlying sadness, a persistent irritation.

What we are encountering is not pathology. It is not depression, laziness, or some personal failing. It is the cumulative effect of decades spent tending to the needs of others—children, partners, parents, careers—

without reserving sufficient space for our inner lives. It is the sensation that arises when a woman reaches her edge of tolerance for what can no longer be carried in silence.

This is the invisible weight. Because we live in a culture that overvalues youth and productivity, many women feel ashamed of their inner shift toward discomfort. We are told to "stay positive," "stay active," "stay relevant." But emotional mastery begins with truth-telling. And the truth is that many of us are exhausted—yes physically, and also emotionally and spiritually. We are tired of pretending. We are tired of managing everyone else's needs. We are tired of being strong.

There is no reason to be ashamed of our fatigue. In fact, it may be the doorway to something profound.

This sensation—the heaviness, the vague unrest—is not a detour. It is the path. It is the signal that something in us is ready to be heard, perhaps for the first time in decades. This is where emotional fitness begins: not with a reinvention of the self, but with a radical listening to who you've always been.

THE RECLAMATION OF SELF

The invisible weight that a woman carries in her sixties is not just the residue of care, responsibility, and performance—it is also the erosion of the self she left unattended. And yet, beneath her fatigue, beneath her disillusionment and disorientation, something ancient and powerful begins to stir: the desire to come home to herself.

This is the reclamation. It does not arrive with drama or fanfare. It does not require a reinvention or a grand life overhaul. Instead, it begins with a single, courageous question: *What would it mean to live the life that is mine?*

For decades, many of us organize our identities around usefulness. We have been needed, so we have belonged. But in the absence of that daily need or in choosing not to prioritize it anymore for entirely personal reasons that are nobody else's effing business, we are invited into a different kind of belonging with our friends and family and random strangers—one that is not transactional, but rooted in presence.

We begin to reclaim our:

- **Time.** Our actions are no longer allocated by obligation, but by desire.

- **Voices.** They are raised not for validation, but to express our truth.

- **Inner lives.** These are not hidden behind roles, but brought forward as central.

Reclamation can be uncomfortable. It also may be lonely, at least at first, until we meet other authentic women we can have fun hanging around with who are vibrant and engaged and are breaking away from their old molds. The roles we formerly chose to play were exhausting although they were familiar and gave shape to our days. Now, the shape must come from within. But what a privilege it is to live long enough to become who we truly are.

IDENTITY AS ESSENCE, NOT ROLE

In our earlier decades, identity is often performative. As children, we learn how to be acceptable, how to be valuable, how to succeed within the structures we inherit. From then on, even our most intimate choices—such as what to wear, how to speak, what activities to pursue—were shaped by subtle, sometimes invisible forces of social approval and expectation.

But in this chapter of life, a new possibility emerges: the opportunity to shed performance and arrive at essence.

Essence is not what you do. It is what remains when you stop "doing." It is not your job title, your history, or your image. It is your unadorned self. The part of you that does not shift with public opinion or change with your social roles. It is the soul of your presence.

In our sixties, we are no longer tasked with proving ourselves. We are tasked with remembering ourselves. The woman who once worked to be seen now sees herself. The woman who once gave away her energy to belong now reclaims it in service of becoming.

This shift is subtle and radical.

It redefines power not as control, but as alignment.

It redefines beauty not as youth, but as resonance.

It redefines identity not as projection, but as embodiment.

And from this grounded state—one marked by embodiment, resonance, and alignment—life begins to feel different. More spacious. More truthful. More your own.

You may notice you're no longer performing womanhood, but inhabiting it.

No longer chasing meaning, but becoming it.

No longer asking *Who do they need me to be?* but instead, *Who have I always been, beneath it all?*

REFLECTION AND INTEGRATION

A journal invitation for your sovereign self

Reflect and write about the following prompts.

- *What emotions have I habitually avoided or suppressed?*

- *How do I tend to react when I feel unseen or misunderstood?*

- *What would it look like to meet my emotions without judgment?*

THREE

Time as an Ally, not an Adversary

"It is not death that a man should fear, but never beginning to live in accordance with nature."

MARCUS AURELIUS

A woman in her sixties knows something that a younger woman cannot yet fully grasp (or at least I didn't): Time is limited. This awareness, which may once have been frightening to her, becomes something else entirely as she gets older: a liberation.

THE LIBERATION OF THE FINITE

When we are young, we live with the illusion of endlessness. We delay what matters. We tolerate what drains us. We postpone pursuing experiences that call to us. Time feels abundant, so we spend it carelessly—on people, on roles, on proving, on being pleasing. But in the third act of our lives, the illusion lifts. And in its place comes clarity.

23

If you are approaching your seventh decade, you can expect to begin asking different questions, like:

- *With only twenty or thirty years left of life, at most, how do I want to feel in them?*

- *What or whom have I outgrown?*

- *What have I not yet allowed myself to claim?*

- *What desire, identity, truth, or expression have I longed for, but kept at a distance— whether out of fear, conditioning, or the belief that it wasn't "for me"?*

Such questions are not morbid. They are illuminating. They can sharpen your vision and tune your inner ear. Self-inquiry of this sort makes you intolerant of what is false and hungry for what is true.

When time is understood as finite, it's natural to stop performing. You can expect to stop deferring, or to stop spending hours explaining things to people who are not really listening. You will start living from the inside out. This is the gift of aging: Time becomes a compass rather than a threat. Less a countdown than a deepening.

REFRAMING PRODUCTIVITY, REDEFINING WORTH

In a culture that worships speed and celebrates output, many women arrive in their sixties feeling subtly—or overtly—irrelevant. We are praised for our energy, our usefulness, our multitasking prowess throughout our adult lives, but if we begin to slow down or to question the urge for constant doing, we may feel guilty. As if our new stillness is idleness. As if resting signals a decline.

Emotional mastery demands a profound reorientation of our values. We need to move from using productivity as the primary source of our identity toward presence.

You were never meant to be in perpetual motion. You were never meant to define your worth by your ability to produce. You are not a machine. You are a consciousness, a presence, a living intelligence. And you are allowed to exist for your own sake.

This decade offers you the opportunity to claim a rhythm that belongs to you—one that isn't dictated by market forces or family schedules, which honors your internal pace. You may still choose to create, to build, to serve—but the work you do going forward will not be done because your value as a person depends on it.

We're at an age when our identities are being redefined and old roles are falling away. This stage of life may be characterized by career reinvention or retirement, when caretaking of kids ends, maybe caretaking parents ends, too (or begins), and we face health transitions or diagnoses, as well as societal invisibility. So beyond sixty, we are entering a phase where external validation no longer suffices and the inner world demands attention and allegiance. This is an era of depth. Of going deeper perhaps than we ever have before.

You may begin to recognize in your sixties that silence is not emptiness, but rather a form of listening. That rest is not a break from life, but a way into it. That doing less can be a path to becoming more.

Choosing to do less in the average day is not about passivity. This path is about developing discernment— knowing when to act and when to allow. And letting the ordinary moments be rich and full of meaning. It is about redefining your notion of usefulness, so you begin choosing to engage in actions not just for the sake of busyness, but as a matter of resonance. Becoming more concerned with alignment than output.

The woman who has mastered her time no longer asks *What should I be doing?* she asks *What is mine to do now?*

CHOOSING LEGACY OVER MOMENTUM

There comes a moment in a woman's life when achieving momentum no longer feels like a virtue or a worthy goal. Constant motion, once equated with ambition or relevance, begins to feel hollow. In its place arises a desire for something more enduring, more vital: the desire for legacy. Not legacy as fame, financial status, or a monument to an achievement. But legacy as presence. As imprint. As the subtle, yet indelible, impact of a life well lived.

The shift to valuing your vitality more than your accomplishments could be disorienting at first. When you no longer feel the rush to "get ahead," you can expect that the internal drive which has propelled you for decades will begin to quiet. And in that stillness, a different voice will speak. A wiser voice. It will ask:

_ᔐ What do I want to leave behind in the fabric of the world?

_ᔐ What values do I want to embody, model, and transmit from now on?

_ᔐ What parts of myself still long to be expressed before I go?

Legacy is not created in one grand gesture. It is crafted by a thousand subtle choices, such as how you show up in a conversation, how you speak to yourself in solitude, and how you hold space for others without abandoning your own truth.

The woman who lives with legacy in mind moves differently. She's less interested in proving, more devoted to aligning. She's no longer seduced by urgency. She's loyal to what is meaningful. She has nothing to prove and much to give.

And while legacy is what lingers after we're gone, it is shaped moment by moment in how we live now— through our choices, our presence, and our impact. What endures in others may be our words, our work, our example—but more often, it will be the steady truth of how we treated them, and how fully we inhabited our lives while we had them.

LIVING WITH URGENCY, BUT WITHOUT ANXIETY

There is a difference—a subtle, but profound difference—between living with urgency and living with anxiety. Urgency can be grounded in presence, but it does not have to be rooted in fear. Anxiety scatters. Urgency clarifies. Anxiety whispers, "There's not enough time." Urgency declares, "This moment matters."

As we move into and through our sixties, our awareness of time's finitude will stop being purely theoretical. As we face change and loss, we can expect them to become embodied. But change and loss need not be sources of dread. Awareness of impermanence can be a source of power.

In our sixties, ideally we begin to feel a deep pull toward what is essential. We lose patience for the performative, the petty, the redundant. We feel called to move through life with fewer filters, fewer apologies, and more truth. Believing important matters need to be addressed without delay is not about rushing. It is about precision. It is about making each moment count—not out of panic, but out of reverence. Urgency, in its purest form, is an act of devotion. It's not just pressure; it's clarity. It arises when something in us knows *This matters now.* In those moments, we are moved to act. To speak the thing we've delayed. To show up without rehearsing. To choose without apology.

Urgency compels us to say:

⟲ *I will not wait to speak my mind.*

⟲ *I will not delay my joy.*

⟲ *I will not postpone the life I came here to live.*

When a woman learns to walk with time as her ally, she no longer fears the clock. She does not shrink from the years ahead; she deepens into them. She understands that every day is a vessel, and she chooses to fill it with meaning rather than noise.

Emotional mastery in motion is to live:

⟲ With urgency, but without anxiety.

⟲ With purpose, not performance.

⟲ Fully, on your own terms, while time is still yours to shape.

REFLECTION AND INTEGRATION

A journal invitation for your sovereign self

Write about the following prompts.

↩ *What am I grieving that I haven't fully acknowledged?*

↩ *Which old identities or roles am I being called to release?*

↩ *What loss has unexpectedly deepened my strength?*

PART TWO

THE EMOTIONAL
ECOSYSTEM

FOUR

Relationships in the Third Act

"Associate with people who are likely to improve you."

SENECA

The relationships that carried us through earlier chapters of life may not be the ones that accompany us through this one. And that is not a failure—it is an evolution.

INTIMACY WITHOUT ENMESHMENT

In our sixties, the architecture of connection begins to shift. What once felt obligatory begins to feel optional. What once was tolerated is gently—though sometimes abruptly—released. Our increasing emotional mastery in this period brings with it the typically new requirement that, for us, intimacy must be mutual, rather than a one-sided performance done to get someone's approval—occurring in circumstances that are nourishing rather than depleting.

For many women, this shift in emphasis within their relationships is the first time in their lives that they are able to distinguish closeness from enmeshment. In earlier decades, emotional entanglement often masqueraded as love. Merging identities with a romantic partner, attempting to manage others' moods, absorbing responsibility that was never truly theirs— these patterns were normalized, even rewarded. But now, the cost of emotional overextension seems too high.

As you age, your boundaries and values will become clearer. You will no longer be willing to trade your peace for proximity. You will no longer be willing to conflate sacrifice with connection.

Fortunately, true intimacy does not require you to disappear. It does not demand self-abandonment as proof of devotion. It does not flourish in codependency, in silence, or in subtle self-erasure.

The sixties are the decade wherein many women redefine what *closeness* means. For them, this decade of life ultimately becomes less about:

- Frequency, and more about depth.

- Needing, and more about knowing.

- Managing each other, and more about witnessing each other.

The woman who is emotionally masterful can sit in the presence of another without absorbing their energy, fixing their pain, or reshaping herself to fit their comfort. She knows how to be close with another person without becoming fused with them. She knows how to love without disappearing. This is intimacy without enmeshment. Connection rooted in sovereignty. Love that honors, rather than erases, the self.

FRIENDSHIP, ESTRANGEMENT, AND THE GRACE OF BOUNDARIES

Friendship in our sixties is no longer defined by quantity or frequency. It is defined by resonance. By ease. By the sacred simplicity of being seen without explanation. And yet, this is also the chapter of our lives in which long-held friendships can most easily drift, fracture, or dissolve. Bonds that once felt permanent can begin to fray under the pressure of mismatched values, unspoken resentments, or simply the divergence of emotional growth.

The unraveling of a friendship can be painful, especially when there's history, shared milestones, or a sense of who you used to be together. It can feel like a kind of mourning, even when the ending is mutual— or necessary. But the truth-telling involved in severing ties can be liberating and bring relief. And there is grace in that. You begin to understand that not all relationships are meant to stretch across every season of your life. Some were meant to hold a version of you that no longer exists.

Terminating a relationship that is no longer relevant to your life is not a betrayal of a friend—it's an acknowledgment of your and your friend's personal evolution.

In this stage of emotional mastery, expressing your boundaries is not putting up walls, it is a form of intimacy.

Sharing your boundaries is saying:

⟢ *This is how I care for myself.*

⟢ *This is what allows me to stay open,*
   without depletion.

⟢ *This is what honors the relationship,*
   by keeping it honest.

Some friendships deepen in our sixties—not through effort, but through mutual recognition. Others fade from prominence—not from neglect, but from the realization that they no longer belong. And sometimes, there is complete estrangement because a relationship has reached its limit.

Whichever is the case for you, the end of a relationship is an invitation to release what no longer fits you without anger. To create space for the unexpected. To trust that solitude can be a form of connection—with yourself, with truth, with the kind of relationships that will meet you where you are now. Friendship in this decade is less about history and more about alignment. Less about staying, more about staying real. Less about loyalty to the past, more about integrity in the present. And when a friendship endures at this point in our lives, it won't be out of habit, but out of something far more beautiful: choice.

LOVING WITHOUT OVEREXTENDING

Many women in their sixties arrive at a startling revelation: Love, as they've practiced it, has often meant overreaching. Over accommodating. Over giving. Too often, their love has been conflated with self-erasure—proof of devotion was shown through sacrifice.

But emotional mastery teaches us that love does not require depletion. It does not ask us to carry what was never ours to hold. It does not require the constant translation of our needs into something more palatable.

To love in your third act is to love cleanly. With clear edges. With open hands. It is no longer about losing yourself in the name of connection. It is about anchoring more deeply into yourself while allowing others to do the same in themselves.

In earlier decades, love may have been tinged with anxiety for you. You may have wondered: *Am I enough? Will they leave? What do they need me to be?*

At this age, love is steadier and more sovereign. You'll reflect: *How can I stay true to myself while remaining open to another?* Romantic partnership is no longer about merging; it's about mirroring.

You will begin to reimagine what it means to give:

- Not as rescue, but as presence.

- Not as martyrdom, but as conscious offering.

- Not as duty, but as choice.

At this age, we stop keeping score. Stop explaining our boundaries. Stop tending to others at the expense of ourselves.

This shift can be unsettling for those accustomed to our overextension. You may find your "no" met with confusion. Or your calm detachment mistaken for withdrawal. But what people will be witnessing is not rejection, but your self-reclamation.

If love remains—whether it be romantic, familial, or platonic—in your sixties it does so not because you've overreached to preserve it, but because it has evolved to meet you where you are: whole, awake, and no longer willing to leave yourself behind in the name of being loved.

REFLECTION AND INTEGRATION

A journal invitation for your sovereign self

Use the following prompts to write in your journal.

⟟ *Where in my life am I still saying yes when I mean no?*

⟟ *What boundary could I establish that would radically honor my current self?*

⟟ *How has my definition of generosity changed over time?*

FIVE

The Art of Emotional Curation

*"We are more often frightened than hurt; and we
suffer more in imagination than in reality."*

SENECA

By the time we reach our sixties we have earned
the right to choose with precision. No longer
driven by social obligation, ambition, or
performance, we are free to become curators of our
own emotional ecosystems. And yet, many of us
struggle with our newfound freedom—not because we
lack clarity, but because we've been conditioned to
ignore it.

DISCERNMENT OVER DEFAULT

For much of our lives, we allocated our emotional
energy to different things by default. We gave because
we were expected to. We stayed because it was easier
than leaving. We engaged because silence felt

41

awkward. We tolerated because we didn't want to offend.

But now, the invitation is different. We have developed the inner fortitude to choose with discernment rather than from obligation. Discernment is a refined form of judgment—clarity born from self-respect. It is not cold—it is precise. It is the intelligence that says, "This conversation no longer nourishes me." "This commitment no longer aligns with who I am."

"This dynamic costs me more than I can afford to give."

The woman who practices emotional mastery does not scatter her energy. She invests it.

She does not say yes out of fear or no out of anger. She chooses from her center.

Exercising your discernment is not selfish. It is sacred. Discernment allows you to:

_◎ Withdraw without guilt.

_◎ Engage without performing.

_◎ Remain open without being porous.

The art of emotional curation is shaping a life that reflects your inner truth, as well as your inherited roles. It is to no longer default to what has always been, but to ask—boldly, tenderly, repeatedly: *What belongs now?*

CHOOSING WHAT—AND WHO—
BELONGS TO YOU

In this chapter of life, inclusion is no longer automatic. It is intentional. You will begin to look at your relationships, commitments, even your thoughts, through the eyes of a curator—someone not in search of perfection, but coherence. What aligns stays. What no longer fits you—no matter how long it's been part of your life—may need to be gently or decisively released.

Discernment is the subtle skill of emotional mastery: being able to differentiate between what you've outgrown and what still nourishes you. It can be difficult, even disorienting, to acknowledge that someone or something you once loved no longer belongs in your inner circle.

But belonging is not based on the longevity of a relationship. It is a gift bestowed by resonance.

In your sixties, you will begin to ask:

_9 *Does this person energize or exhaust me?*

_9 *Does this belief serve who I am now, or is it a remnant of who I once needed to be?*

_9 *Is this habit truly mine, or something I inherited without question?*

Letting go of things that no longer serve or please does not necessarily require dramatic exits or public declarations. Sometimes, it can be accomplished simply by the withdrawal of energy, the choosing not to engage, or a graceful shift in proximity. But sometimes, the act of letting go must be more definitive. An overt boundary must be drawn, a pattern broken, a relationship released directly, face to face, with a declaration of intent.

Curation does not mean creating a sterile, rigid life devoid of complexity. It means shaping an inner world that reflects your values, your growth, and your truth. You are no longer the keeper of everyone else's comfort. You are the steward of your own clarity. To choose what—and who—belongs is not a rejection of others. It is an act of allegiance to yourself.

MAKING PEACE WITH IMPERMANENCE

Curation, by its very nature, involves imper-manence. It is the practice of choosing not only what to include, but when to let go of things you do not wish to include. In your sixties, you will find that letting go becomes an essential and often repeated act—letting go not just of people and possessions, but of ideas, expectations, and former selves.

Letting go is not always easy. Even when we are clear-eyed about what no longer fits, we may still feel the ache of release. We may grieve the version of ourselves who once needed *that* friendship, *that* role, *that* dream. We may wrestle with the sadness of recognizing that this thing has run its course.

But emotional mastery teaches us that imper-manence is not a flaw in the design of life. It *is* the design. And when we stop resisting that truth, we begin to see endings differently. Not as failures, but as transitions. Not as losses, but as refinements. Impermanence becomes a companion—not the thief of stability, but the catalyst of clarity. You will soon trust that what falls away is making space for what is more aligned. You will begin to feel less tethered to nostalgia and more loyal to presence.

Yes, there are things you'll never get back.

Yes, there are people you still miss.

Yes, some seasons ended before you were ready.

But there is also this: a new spaciousness. A deeper trust. A self you could not have accessed until you let go. The art of emotional curation in its most refined form is the graceful, sovereign act of choosing what remains and honoring what has passed—without turning away from either.

REFLECTION AND INTEGRATION

A journal invitation for your sovereign self

Reflect on the following questions to identify patterns in your relationships, define what true connection means to you, and consider specific ways you can bring more integrity into how you engage with others.

_⑨_ *What does soul-level connection feel like to me now?*

_⑨_ *Which relationships truly nourish me, and which drain me?*

_⑨_ *How can I be more honest in showing up for others?*

SIX

The Liberation of Joy

"Very little is needed to make a happy life;
it is all within yourself."

MARCUS AURELIUS

There is a persistent myth in our society that joy belongs to the young. That delight is the domain of those still full of future. That play is frivolous. And that aging gracefully means becoming more muted, more modest, more invisible. But it should be ignored. Acting muted to honor a social convention is suppressive. It's not the same as being quiet. Quiet can be potent. It can be presence without performance. Muteness, by contrast, is what happens when we shrink to fit someone else's expectation.

This myth is not just a cultural lie; it's an act of erasure. A sovereign woman may be quiet, but she can never be erased.

RECLAIMING DESIRE, PLAY, AND SELF-EXPRESSION

We need to reclaim play and self-expression. Joy is not a reward for youth. It is a right of being. Desire is not undignified, it's vital. As researchers like psychiatrist Stuart Brown, M.D., and social worker Brené Brown, Ph.D., have shown, play is not a frivolous escape. Rather, it is a portal into joy, connection, and creative resilience. It is a demon-stration, in many ways, of emotional intelligence. Retaining the ability to play as an adult reveals our high intelligence.

In our sixties, joy becomes something entirely different from what it was in our youth. It's less performative and more personal. Less about adrenaline and more about aliveness. It arises not from seeking stimulation, but from cultivating resonance.

If you're like most women, at this age, you will begin to ask yourself not *What should I be doing?* but *What makes me feel most fully myself?*

And often, your own answers will surprise you. You may say things like:

⟲ Unstructured time.

⟲ Solitude.

⟲ Music played "too loud."

⟲ A long-forgotten creative pursuit.

꩜ A color that makes you feel "unreasonably" joyous.

꩜ A book that gives you language for something you've always known.

Embracing these things is not indulgence. It is spiritual hygiene. To reclaim joy in your sixties is to declare that your life is not winding down, it's *refining*. If you can remember that you are not done expressing, creating, becoming, you will reject the narrative that says your role in society now is to disappear quietly and gracefully into the background.

You do not need permission from anyone else to live with delight. You only need to remember that joy is not a distraction from a serious life. Rather, it is what makes a serious life worth living.

LIVING WITH DELIGHT AS A COUNTER-NARRATIVE TO DECLINE

Aging women are surrounded by subtle and not-so-subtle messages that suggest our aging is a diminishment. That joy, sensuality, excitement, and wonder are best left to the young—or at the very least, that they must be tempered with restraint in later life.

This attempted social conditioning is not just oppressive. It is incorrect. The pursuit of joy, when intentionally practiced in our sixties, is not naïve, but radical. It is a counternarrative. A refusal. A reclamation.

It is how we declare:

_⚲ *I will not shrink into cultural invisibility.*

_⚲ *I will not numb myself with duty, fatigue, or cynicism.*

_⚲ *I will not live only in the past, or only for others.*

Choosing delight becomes a form of resistance—a soft, luminous protest against the assumption that your inner world is fading. It reminds you that vibrancy is not something you wear on your skin, but something you carry in your gaze. That vitality is not about pace, but presence. It's not the emotion alone that defies expectation, but the decision to lean into it. To prioritize beauty, pleasure, and play. To let yourself glow without justification.

After sixty, you can expect to begin taking joy seriously—not in the sense of controlling it, but in honoring its place in your life. After sixty, you no longer chase joy; you actively cultivate it. You build your days around it, rather than waiting to experience it until after everything else is done. You stop waiting for someone else to create joy for you. You create opportunities for joy everywhere you go all the time.

And as joy reenters and then fills your entire body from head to toe—not as a reward, but as a practice or spiritual ritual—you will realize something essential:

You were not designed simply to manage your life. You were meant to revel in it.

Delight is not frivolous.

Pleasure is not extravagant.

Reveling is the emotional and spiritual nourishment that will sustain your third act.

To live with delight is to declare *I am still here. I am still becoming. And I still choose wonder.*

THE RADICAL ACT OF BEING FULLY ALIVE

In your sixties, joy stops being a fleeting feeling and becomes a state of alignment. It is what happens when your outer life reflects your inner truth. When you no longer perform, suppress, or justify, but allow yourself simply to live.

This—in our culture and era—is radical.

To be a woman in her sixties who is emotionally sovereign, unapologetically joyful, and deeply alive is to stand in defiance of everything we were taught to become. We were told to be agreeable. To stay small. To age gently, invisibly, quietly.

But now you know that joy is not a luxury or a reward. It is your birthright. Even so, claiming the things that bring you joy may require an act of courage.

Courageous expressions of joy are not giddy or performative. Curate joyful moments for an audience of one: yourself. Let them be rich, textured, and deeply personal.

Joy often arises in the smallest of moments, such as:

- Morning light across the kitchen table.
- The pause in a meaningful conversation.
- A private laugh that no one else hears.
- A return to your body after years of detachment.

Being fully alive does not mean being relentlessly happy. It means being relentlessly awake. It means allowing yourself to feel—without rushing, numbing, or shrinking. It means remembering that experiencing joy is neither irresponsible nor indulgent, but a vital signal of wholeness.

To feel joy in a world that tries to rob you of it is not a denial of pain. It is a refusal to be defined by it.

To live with joy in your sixties is to live with intent, elegance, and power. It is to say, without words "I am still here. I am still luminous. And my light will not be dimmed."

REFLECTION AND INTEGRATION

A journal invitation for your sovereign self

Use the following questions to reconnect with your sources of joy, pleasure, and vitality. Explore where you might be limiting your own experience of beauty, and then consider ways to expand your capacity for delight on your own terms—authentically.

_ɔ_ *What truly lights me up regardless of anyone else's opinion?*

_ɔ_ *When was the last time I felt joyful for no reason?*

_ɔ_ *How could I expand my capacity to receive pleasure and beauty?*

PART THREE

MASTERY IN MOTION

SEVEN

The Practice of Stillness

*"The body should be treated more rigorously, that it
may not be disobedient to the mind."*

SENECA

In earlier stages of life, silence was often seen as a
void—something to be filled, avoided, even feared.
In our sixties, silence becomes something else
entirely: a sanctuary. A teacher. A mirror.

SILENCE AS A SOURCE OF INSIGHT

Stillness is not the absence of life; it's the presence
of depth. It is where you hear the truth underneath the
noise. That's why, in a culture addicted to speed and
spectacle, the choice to cultivate stillness is sub-
versive. To your nervous system, it says: "I will not race
through my days. I will not mistake urgency for
importance. I will not outsource my knowing."

To be still is to return to yourself, again and again, until your own presence becomes the most trustworthy voice in the room.

Removing yourself so you can be still in private is not about detaching from the world. It is about becoming anchored enough in yourself to engage with the world more intentionally.

Stillness sharpens your discernment. It softens your reactivity. It gives you back to yourself. Even five minutes of conscious quietude—free from distraction, free from performance—can return you to your center.

Taking a moment to center in stillness is not laziness. This is listening.

This is not inactivity. It's alignment.

The woman who practices stillness—whether through meditation, journaling, or sitting on a park bench—does not seek her answers from the external. She knows wisdom rises from within.

Eventually, she no longer fills space to prove she belongs. She no longer speaks to make others comfortable. She lets her silence speak for her when words are too small for what she knows.

Her stillness is emotional mastery in its most refined form: the capacity to remain rooted while the world keeps spinning.

CREATING EMOTIONAL SPACIOUSNESS

Stillness is not just the absence of noise; it's also the cultivation of spaciousness. And emotional spaciousness is a skill, an art, and, for many women in their sixties, a revelation. For decades, we've been trained to fill the gaps between people, between plans, between emotions. As a result, we'll try to smooth over awkwardness, bridge silences, manage discomfort, and preempt need. We tend. We respond. We hyperfunction.

But now, there is room for something different. Emotional spaciousness allows you to let a moment breathe before rushing to fix it. To let a relationship evolve without forcing resolution. To sit with your own discomfort without demanding immediate relief. This is not neglect. It is refinement. It comes from understanding that not all tensions must be solved, not all feelings explained, not all conversations completed.

Spaciousness allows your inner world to expand beyond the binary thinking of right or wrong, success or failure, joy or despair. It opens the door to complexity. To nuance. To grace.

When you cultivate emotional spaciousness, you begin to notice yourself:

- Speaking more slowly, and meaning more when you do.

- Listening without strategizing your response.

⁀◯ Making fewer assumptions, and feeling less pressure to perform.

This is where your emotional mastery could become visible to you—not in any dramatic transformation, but in a gentle, yet profound shift you're making to let life unfold without attempting to control its every detail.

In the space of allowance, you will find your genuine self. Not the self that is shaped by your roles or reactions, but the one who simply is.

Your genuine self is a grounded, open, sovereign being.

BECOMING FLUENT IN YOUR INNER WORLD

The deepest expression of emotional mastery is not how well we manage others; it's how intimately we know ourselves. This level of intimacy is only possible when we've made space for stillness, silence, and self-inquiry.

In her sixties, a woman's need to understand herself becomes more urgent. She seeks awareness not for the sake of fixing or optimizing, but for the sake of *inhabiting.* To be in full residence within her own being.

Becoming fluent in your inner world means learning the language of your emotions, your instincts, your rhythms. It means no longer feeling as if you need to explain your feelings to justify their existence. It means knowing the difference between intuition and fear, between tiredness and depletion, between longing and avoidance. This fluency gives rise to emotional sovereignty. This age is when you can stop outsourcing your clarity. You can stop performing self-awareness for others.

In my experience, many women appear emotionally evolved—using all the "right" language associated with growth and insight—who remain disconnected from their actual experience. They might say they've "let go" of something, although it's still eating them alive. They might act compassionate on the outside, while secretly seething. These women are playing the part of the self-aware woman instead of doing the actual inner work they need to do.

Their behavior isn't motivated by a desire to fool people; it's often subconscious. There is a lot of pressure on us to look emotionally intelligent even when we're struggling. A name for this kind of performance (which really is about a woman fooling herself) is *spiritual bypassing.*

It's performative calm. It's wisdom as performance.

As you become an emotionally sovereign woman, the performances end. You simply *know* what you need, what you're willing to offer and what you're no longer available for.

Because you have stopped trying to be impressively wise, you may:

   ◯ Begin to journal—not to report your findings
   to others, but to reveal yourself to yourself.

61

_⊙ Sit in meditation—not to escape thought,
   but to meet yourself within it.

_⊙ Walk, breathe, pause—not as routine, but
   as ritual.

Remember, immersion in your inner world is not indulgence. It will help you experience your own presence.

The act or practice of turning inward, being with your own emotions, thoughts, and truth in a sustained, intentional way is not isolation. It is an act of communion with your true self.

When a woman becomes fluent in her inner world, she moves through the outer world with quiet certainty. She does not chase clarity—it accompanies her. She does not wait for approval—she has nothing to prove. She does not seek direction—she listens, and she knows.

The gift of stillness is not emptiness, but embodiment.

Not withdrawal, but return.

Not silence, but fluency in your own sacred language.

THE STILL POINT IN THE STORM

There is a moment—subtle, almost imperceptible—when stillness no longer feels like absence, but like power.

Many of us reach our sixties having spent decades in forward motion. We've moved through lives shaped by caretaking, achievement, self-management, and relentless proving. So when stillness first *truly* arrives the pause can feel disorienting. Not just because it's unfamiliar, but because it strips away the noise that once anchored us. We may begin to ask *Who am I without the momentum?*

Within that pause lies a portal. Stillness is not what happens when activity stops. It is what remains when the unnecessary falls away. It is the still point in the storm, the eye within the whirlwind, a place where clarity takes root—not in spite of the chaos, but because we have chosen to meet it from within.

And while the world may continue to spin, we do not have to spin with it.

THE SOVEREIGN NERVOUS SYSTEM

Stillness is not resistance to life. It is a sacred stance we take within our lives. It is how we declare "I will no longer be swept away by every urgency, opinion, or invitation. I will be deliberate in how I respond, how I show up, and who I become."

One of the most radical outcomes of cultivating stillness is the regulation of the nervous system—not through force, but through familiarity. As women, we are often socialized into states of hypervigilance—of attunement run amok. We scan the room for emotional signals, try to anticipate other people's needs before they're voiced, brace ourselves for rejection or demand. Over time, we turn our vigilance inward. Even in our silence, we remain on alert. But authentic stillness interrupts the nervous system's habit of bracing.

As your breath deepens, your body begins to remember what safety feels like. Your shoulders may drop, not because someone told them to, but because something in you feels, for the first time in a long while, that it's safe to soften.

You're not preparing for impact; you're living without flinching.

A sovereign nervous system is not one that "never gets activated." It's one that knows how to return to calm. In our sixties, stillness becomes the pathway we take back to center. We choose to be still not as a punishment for losing our shit, but as a preferred practice. Stillness is a place where our safety is rebuilt not from certainty, but from presence.

In a calm state, your reactions will soften. Your boundaries clarify. You will be able to recognize—perhaps at long last—the difference between real threats and inherited fears. And in this recognition, you will begin to respond rather than react to things that stimulate and activate. The ability to regulate your nervous system is not just a sign of emerging emotional mastery, it's a demonstration of your physiological sovereignty.

PROTECTING THE SACRED QUIET

Stillness, once it has been cultivated, must be protected. Not because it is fragile, but because the world will constantly try to pull you away from it. Notifications. Expectations. The invisible labor of being a woman in a world that equates stillness with irrelevance. These are the challenges that can pull you from your calm center.

If you've reached your sixties, you now know better than to bite the lures cast in your direction. You know that stillness is not the absence of mattering, but the deepening of meaning.

That is why you protect your quiet personal time.

You protect the sacred quiet not with defensiveness, but with discernment. You create rituals around your mornings or your evenings. You become intentional about who has access to your energy. You pause before responding. You resist urgency, not because you are indifferent, but because you are anchored. And you begin to notice how much noise was never yours to hold.

Protecting your quiet is not a celebration of withdrawal. This is boundary setting.

This is not selfishness. This is stewardship.

You are not shutting the world out. You are inviting yourself in.

THE FEMININE WISDOM OF THE PAUSE

There is a deep, ancient rhythm within us—one most of us were never taught to trust. It is the rhythm of the pause. The inhale before the exhale. The waiting before the answer. The dormancy before the bloom. And in stillness, we can reconnect with this inner cadence.

When we are aligned with this rhythm, we stop expecting ourselves to perform clarity.

We start allowing our wisdom to unfold in its own time. We unlearn urgency as a virtue.

This is a feminine rhythm, because it isn't linear. It spirals. It circles. It flows. It gestates.

Stillness becomes a way of listening to this rhythm. Of not rushing the insights. Of not forcing the resolution. Of honoring the sacred gestation period between question and knowing.

In your sixties, you will come to understand that not every pause is a problem. Some are holy.

WEAVING STILLNESS INTO ORDINARY LIFE

Eventually, stillness becomes less of a practice and more of a design principle. As we mature and become emotionally masterful, it's common for women to begin to shape their lives around it—not to avoid participation, but to ensure alignment.

Perhaps you have already attained the state wherein you let go of commitments that fracture your energy and gravitate toward relationships that respect silence.

You may notice in this decade that your home, your calendar, your inner monologue have all begun to shift. You may find yourself:

- Lighting a candle in the morning.
- Pausing to breathe before answering the phone.
- Writing a note to your future self, not because you're lost, but because you've arrived.

If so, then stillness has become a thread woven through your days. Not dramatic. Not performative. Just present.

In the design of your life, a truth emerges—not loud, but certain: Being present with your genuine thoughts and feelings is not just what you do for practice. A genuine being is who you are becoming.

REFLECTION AND INTEGRATION

A journal invitation for your sovereign self

Reflect honestly on your current beliefs, bodily awareness, and emotional patterns. Use these questions to identify where outdated stories or unresolved shame may still be shaping your experience—and where new possibilities for self-compassion could emerge.

_⁀_ *What have I believed about aging that no longer serves me?*

_⁀_ *How do I relate to my body now, whether it's in stillness or in motion?*

_⁀_ *Where does shame live in my body, and what does it need to heal?*

EIGHT

The Power of Emotional Inquiry

"Silence is a lesson learned through life's many sufferings."

SENECA

One of the most profound shifts that comes with emotional mastery is moving from judgment and opinion to curiosity.

CURIOSITY AS A GATEWAY TO CLARITY

In earlier decades, you may have instinctively labeled your feelings, calling them too much, not enough, irrational, or inconvenient. You may have rushed to fix, suppress, or justify them. But in your sixties, you will see that your emotions are not problems to solve. That they are information. Invitations. Portals into deeper knowing.

Isn't it beautiful that when you pause long enough to listen to your feelings, without rushing to interpret or repair them, a new kind of clarity forms? For instance, you might recognize that anger is a boundary crying out to be honored. Or that your sorrow is pointing to a desire as yet unlived. Or that your joy, too, is information: a breadcrumb leading you home to your natural wisdom. Curiosity doesn't just soften judgment; it also reveals meaning. It gives your emotions somewhere to go.

Curiosity is what transforms the chaos of emotion into clarity. Instead of asking *Why am I feeling this again?* you can ask *What is this feeling here to show me?*

That said, emotional inquiry requires presence and precision. To gain clarity, you must learn to sit with discomfort—not to punish yourself, but to listen to what the discomfort has to say. You also must learn to explore joy—not to hold on to it, but to understand what nourishes it. This form of inquiry is not about over analysis. Nor is it about intellectualizing every flicker of feeling.

Clarity comes from allowing yourself to engage with your emotional life with neutral curiosity, rather than be ruled by it or alienated from it.

To tame the chaos of your emotions, stop framing your emotions as enemies. Stop measuring your value by how "together" you seem. Ask more and better questions. In doing so, you will receive better answers.

Curiosity opens you. It softens defensiveness. It sharpens discernment. And most importantly, it grants you access to yourself. Not the curated version, but the real one.

NAMING, WITNESSING, AND INTEGRATING EMOTION

For much of our lives, we were expected to manage our emotions rather than to understand them. We've been told to "get over it," "stay strong," or "let it go" — as though our emotions were an obstacle to overcome rather than a language to be learned.

But emotional mastery does not come from control. It comes from integration. And the first step in achieving integration is *naming*.

When you name what you feel with precision—for example, recognizing that you are experiencing grief, not just sadness, or resentment, not just irritation—it is possible to create space for the named emotion to unfold, inform you, and eventually shift.

The second step is *witnessing.*

This is the practice of observing your emotions without collapsing into them. It is the ability to feel deeply without becoming consumed. For example, as a witness, you watch your anger rise, not with shame, but with presence. You allow your sorrow to speak, not to define you, but to reveal you.

71

The final step in this process is integration. This is where the emotion no longer exists as a separate force, demanding attention or reaction from you. It has become part of your inner landscape—something understood, honored, and whole.

Naming. Witnessing. Integrating. These are the tools of the sovereign woman.

The sovereign woman in her sixties does not flinch at her emotional complexity. She does not seek to be emotionally tidy. She allows her feelings to shape her—not into something weaker or softer than she actually is, which would be a lie and a betrayal of her essence, but into someone clearer, truer, more awake than she was in the past.

Through the practice of emotional integration, a woman becomes less reactive and more responsive. Less driven by patterns and more attuned to presence. Less defined by emotion and more in relationship with it.

She is no longer at the mercy of what she feels. She is in communion with it—and feels fluid, grounded, and free.

REWRITING INTERNAL SCRIPTS WITH PRECISION AND COMPASSION

Every woman carries an internal narrative, a script written in part by her childhood, culture, family, and experiences. Parts of it may be healthy and helpful. But other parts not so much.

Our internal narratives often go unquestioned for decades, even if they are unhelpfully shaping how we love, how we lead, how we limit ourselves.

Some scripted ideas are obvious.

I must always be useful.

I can't show weakness.

If I speak the truth, I will be rejected.

Others are more obscured.

I'm too much.

I'm not enough.

It's too late.

Fortunately, our sixties offer us a sacred opportunity to examine our inner scripts with clear eyes and rewrite damaging sections of them with precision and compassion.

Rewriting a script is not about speaking affirmations. It's not about surface-level positivity. It's not about denying what has hurt you. Rewriting a script is about truth telling. It's about identifying the lies that have shaped your decisions. It's about replacing those lies with new language rooted in self-recognition and emotional sovereignty.

When you notice yourself feeling held back by an idea of limitation, seize the opportunity to ask:

- *Whose voice is this?*

- *Do I still believe this?*

- *What would I say to a beloved friend who held this belief about herself?*

And then, with intention, you can begin to write a new, more supportive script that speaks directly to who you are now.

Teach yourself to believe:

- *My presence is enough.*

- *I am allowed to disappoint others if it means honoring myself.*

- *I will no longer abandon myself to make others comfortable.*

- *It is not too late. I am right on time.*

The process of integrating a powerful new belief is not linear. It also is not always elegant. But in the end, life is not about perfection, it's about liberation.

Rewriting our internal scripts is an act of reclamation of our sovereignty. It will be how the woman you have become takes the pen from the world and says, "I'll take it from here."

THE SOVEREIGN SELF

REFLECTION AND INTEGRATION

A journal invitation for your sovereign self

Explore how quiet moments can nourish you. Use the following questions to discover new ways of welcoming peace, presence, and spaciousness into your life.

⤵ *What is the difference between being alone and being lonely?*

⤵ *Where can I welcome more stillness into my life without guilt?*

⤵ *What do I hear in the silence that I can't hear in the noise?*

NINE

Tending the Body, Honoring the Self

"A fit body, a calm mind, a house full of love.
These things cannot be bought—they must be
earned."

NAVAL RAVIKANT

There is a rarely spoken grief that comes with chronic pain and illness—a grief not just for the loss of the body you once had, but for the ease you once felt moving through the world. When the body becomes unpredictable, as it often does once women reach their sixties, it doesn't just limit your physical capacity, it can also challenge your identity, your confidence, and even your sense of safety in your own skin. When that happens, it may be time to revisit the relationship you have with your body—not to judge it, but to reclaim it with reverence, tenderness, and renewed respect.

THE BODY AS A LIVING ARCHIVE

As aging women, we will experience a range of complaints that is all but inevitable. You may or may not have experienced significant bodily changes yet.

The thing for everyone to know is that living with ongoing discomfort is an invisible labor. It demands a constant negotiation between hope and disappointment, between agency and surrender. And while others may see resilience in the person persisting through physical ailments, what they don't see is the exhaustion of carrying pain through daily life while still trying to show up, to engage, to contribute, to smile. This emotional burden is compounded by how often it is misunderstood or dismissed—especially for women, especially as we age.

There can be shame, too, when we feel unwell. Shame for needing rest. Shame for canceling plans. Shame for not bouncing back. Even the language of "pushing through" can feel violent when what's really needed is gentleness, validation, and space to feel all the things we've been taught to hide: among them, anger, grief, fear, and profound loneliness.

To tend the body as it ages is not just to treat symptoms. It is to bear witness to the emotional cost to a person's spirit of surviving inside a body that does not always cooperate, that no longer moves or heals the way it used to. Honoring yourself in this context means naming that struggle—and choosing, still, to offer your body compassion over criticism. To stop demanding a return to normal and begin creating a new language of reverence for what this body, even now, carries you through.

By our sixties, the body ceases to be neutral. It becomes politicized, pathologized, and scrutinized—by culture, by medicine, and sometimes even by us. But beneath all of that, the body is something more profound: a living archive of our existence.

Let's acknowledge that your body has carried you across decades of adaptation. It has absorbed every loss, every decision, every unspeakable moment of endurance. It remembers what the mind forgets. It holds not just your history, but your unspoken truths.

This is not poetry. This is reality.

And yet, despite all it has done for us—despite what it continues to manage, contain, signal—the aging body is so often met with critique or dismissal. We are urged to correct it, ignore it, outperform it. To treat its changes as malfunctions rather than as data.

But emotional sovereignty invites us to establish a different kind of relationship with our bodies. Not romanticization. Not detachment.

Instead: presence.

This is the age of reckoning with the physical self. Not in the pursuit of youth, but in the pursuit of integrity.

Can you listen to your body without immediately trying to fix it?

Can you witness its decline without collapsing into despair or denial?

Can you experience physical vulnerability without losing access to your power?

These are not abstract questions. They are daily inquiries—especially for the woman who is facing chronic pain, hormonal upheaval, fatigue, or a diagnosis that has reshaped her understanding of her vitality.

Aging in a human body is not simply about acceptance of limitation and loss of functionality. It is about learning how to stay in relationship with something that is changing beneath you, without warning, without your consent. That requires courage.

That requires grace.

That requires a kind of sovereignty that is embodied rather than conceptual.

CHRONIC PAIN AND THE LIMITS OF CONTROL

There is a kind of pain that never fully leaves.

It does not flare and resolve. It lingers.

It shapes the rhythm of your days and the quality of your nights.

It inserts itself into every plan, every movement, every quiet hope for ease.

Chronic pain—whether visible or invisible—is not simply a physical experience. It is existential. It erodes energy, interrupts intimacy, undermines identity. It can shrink your world in ways that others, even those who love you, may never fully understand. And the most disorienting part of it isn't always the pain itself. It's the relentless effort to manage it, to explain it, to prove that it's real.

If you experience chronic pain, you may find yourself caught between resignation and resistance. Resignation feels like surrendering to a life you didn't choose. Resistance feels like constant vigilance, a war against your own body.

But emotional mastery offers a third way, neither passive nor combative: relationship. To be in relationship with chronic pain—or with an acute injury that dramatically disrupts your life for a while, such as a sprained ankle—is to allow it a seat at the table without letting it lead you.

It is the practice of acknowledging your limits without collapsing into them.

Relating to pain involves learning to ask not *How do I get rid of this?* but *How do I live with this and still remain whole?*

This doesn't mean glorifying pain or denying its impact. It means being willing to grieve what you've lost—your mobility, spontaneity, and certain lost versions of yourself—without making the grief you feel about the loss your identity.

You begin to cultivate new kinds of strength, like:

_◯ The strength to ask for help without shame.

_ℒ_ The strength to say no without explanation.

_ℒ_ The strength to rest as a necessity.

As we age, we do well to let go of the mythology of the body as a project—something to sculpt, master, or optimize. Instead, we learn to dwell in the body as it is: imperfect, vulnerable, and deeply wise. This is not an easy relationship. But it can be an honest one. And from honesty comes sovereignty—not the fantasy of full control, but the reality of inner authority, even in the presence of pain.

HEALTH AS RELATIONSHIP, NOT PROJECT

For most of our lives, we are taught to treat our health as a task—something to track, optimize, measure, and manage. We become fluent in metrics like weight, blood pressure, bone density, cholesterol, steps, cycles, and calories. Even in wellness culture, the body is treated like a system to perfect, a performance to maintain.

But what happens when the system falters, when the metrics shift? What happens when your health no longer responds to effort in predictable ways?

In our sixties, the body refuses to be managed like a project. It resists tidy narratives. And what it requires most is not relentless control, but renewed relationship.

A relationship implies presence, listening, and respect. It is not about:

_℧_ Perfection. It's about intimacy.

_℧_ Hacking or optimizing. It's about attuning to the body's needs.

_℧_ Bouncing back from illness or injury. It's about being with the body in whatever condition it's in.

Health behaviors that are motivated by external standards, social approval, or punitive self-discipline rather than a genuine relationship with the body are performative. Staying healthy as we age means allowing our care for our bodies to become less performative and more relational. Sooner or later, you will need to work on your balance and your ability to get up from the floor. Without those two things, you are bound to have an accident you can't recover from. In your sixties, you would also do well to learn to eat to nourish your body and to adhere only to restrictions that are appropriately mandated for your specific condition. For instance, you may need to begin lowering your salt intake, limiting sugar, or avoiding certain foods. But the difference now is the motivation behind your choices.

This is what relational care looks like: neither perfection nor rigidity, but respectful listening. You will move to feel good and optimize your body's functions, rather than to punish yourself for some perceived flaw in your physique. You also will allow yourself to rest without guilt. You will ask your body what it needs, not test it to see how much exertion or pain it can endure.

Having an intimate relationship with your body as an older woman means redefining the concept of *strength*. Yes, physical strength matters. Muscle tone, mobility, balance, and endurance are crucial not just for vitality but for independence and confidence. But at this stage of life, strength is no longer about forcing the body into submission. It's not about overriding pain with willpower or pushing past your limits because someone yells, "One more rep." Instead, strength becomes the ability to exert yourself without leaving yourself.

Being intimate with your body means adhering to the discipline of moving with your body, not against it.

Being gentle with your body is not about swapping softness for strength; it's about claiming sovereignty within strength. It means you can build muscle and increase your stamina while also staying supple, attuned, and relaxed. You honor the feedback your body gives you, even when it surprises you, even when it resists. This is how we stay powerful: not by mimicking the rituals of younger bodies, but by mastering the conversation with our own.

Furthermore, the emotionally masterful woman will eventually begin to see maintaining or improving her physical health not as a linear journey, but as a layered dialogue. Some days she will feel vibrant. Some days she will feel diminished. Both experiences are part of the conversation she's having with her body.

Neither defines her worth.

Sovereignty, in the context of staying healthy for as long as possible, is not the absence of struggle, it's the refusal to abandon yourself when you're in the midst of a given struggle. (Even the healthiest of us gets sick or injured on occasion. There's no shame in it.) Sovereignty means choosing to relate to your body not as a thing to be conquered, but as a companion to be heard, honored, and accompanied through change.

Although this may not have been the health narrative we were given as children, it may be the one that frees us from suffering in response to our body's impermanence.

EMBODIED PRESENCE

The ultimate demonstration of respect for your body is not making attempts to heal every symptom or reverse every change associated with its aging. It is displayed through your commitment to presence—making the decision to inhabit your body fully, even as it shifts, even when it aches, even if it no longer feels like familiar ground.

Embodiment is not measured in degrees of comfort and discomfort. It is about residency. You have the option to stay close to your physical self, especially when you are tempted to dissociate or disappear. Your body is a place of wisdom, sensation, and truth—not just in moments of pain or challenge, but in moments of joy, vitality, and ease. Embodiment is the practice of staying connected, of inhabiting your life through breath, sensation, and choice.

To live in your body, as it is, without resentment or detachment, is a radical act. It means walking slower, and with more intention. It means allowing for softness—physical, emotional, and energetic—without shame. And it means feeling pain without identifying with the pain.

The beauty of being a sovereign woman in your sixties is how you no longer treat your body as a résumé of your discipline in the gym or yoga studio, or as a canvas on which others can paint their opinions. You know you need to offer no proof of your hard work, willpower, or worth. You have let go of trying to "earn" value through tight abs or a perfect practice.

You move and train because it feels good or supports your health—not to impress anyone. You stop apologizing for the space you take up. You begin to wear what feels good. You don't move simply to chase a number on the scale. You move to protect your brain. To strengthen your bones. To keep your joints fluid and your blood flowing. To stay vibrant, sharp, and self-sufficient. And yes, you move to feel awake and connected in your own skin.

At this stage, movement is more than a performance; it's also a form of devotion. To your future self. To your right to feel alive.

Especially beautiful is how you return to practices that bring you back into sensation—stretching, breathwork, walking in nature, swimming, dancing, resting. You no longer consider these indulgences. They are expressions of your sovereignty.

And in this space of embodied presence, something shifts. You begin to live from your skin inward. You begin to anchor your emotions not just in your mind, but in your flesh. You begin to experience not just self-awareness, but self-inhabitation.

The simple truth is that you do not have to love every aspect of your body to honor it.

You do not have to be pain free to be present. You do not have to feel radiant to be real.

What matters now is that you are here. With your body. Not managing it, not fixing it—just living in it.

That, in itself, is wholeness.

That, in itself, is sovereignty.

POSTMENOPAUSE AND RECALIBRATION

Postmenopause arrives not with a final exclamation but with a quiet, often disorienting shift. It marks the end of one biological season, yes—but more importantly, it initiates a new interior landscape. And yet, it is rarely spoken of with honesty or nuance.

For many women, menopause is a milestone long since passed by their sixties—yet its ripple effects are still unfolding. Whether it came on gradually, suddenly after surgery, or earlier than expected, menopause marked the end of one biological era. But postmenopause isn't just an aftermath. It is an ongoing recalibration—physical, emotional, and existential.

And yet, this transition is rarely spoken of with honesty or nuance. Too often, women are offered medical statistics and vague reassurances instead of real conversation.

What follows is not a single shift, but a deep internal reshaping. A recalibration of:

_9 Energy.

_9 Desire.

_9 Metabolism.

_9 Mood.

_9 Memory.

_9 Identity.

Not all of these will apply. Some will show up subtly, others unmistakably. But all are invitations—not to return to who you were, but to meet who you are now.

The changes may be subtle or dramatic. Some women experience the cessation of their menstrual cycles, contraception, reproductive pressures as liberation. Others face grief, unpredictability, and the unsettling sense that they no longer recognize the body they live in.

Both experiences are valid. Many women carry both.

THE SOVEREIGN SELF

The years following menopause are a period when
emotional mastery is essential. We need to be able to
name what is real for us without self-criticism. To stop
minimizing the very real physical and emotional effects
of post-menopause, and give ourselves permission to
grieve and adjust as we settle into a new rhythm in our
lives.
Since you went through menopause, you may have
noticed that you have:

   ꧂ A different relationship to your libido. It's not
   entirely gone, but has changed.

   ꧂ Undergone shifts in cognition, sleep,
   temperature, and mood.

   ꧂ Different boundaries—a new sense of what
   your body allows and refuses.

You may also notice a new depth of wisdom
emerging—a deep knowing that no longer needs to be
explained, justified, or second-guessed And this
knowing may be accompanied by a kind of heat—not
hormonal,
but energetic—that begins to rise from within. This heat
is not a sign of physical decline, but of a system-wide
reorientation.
Your aging body deserves reverence, not shame.
The decade after menopause is not a void. It is the
period when you are building a new architecture of self
that will last you the rest of your life.

89

Your life from now on will not be ruled by your reproductive cycle or desire for fertility. It has the potential to be animated by clarity. By intuition. By sovereignty. This intermediate stage of adaptation is not about returning to who you were. It is about learning to live fully as the woman you've become—in relationship to the newly possible.

There's no need to explain, diminish, or decorate the truth of your experience.

You are not past your prime.

You are past the noise.

And what remains may be the deepest power you've ever known.

REFLECTION AND INTEGRATION

A journal invitation for your sovereign self

Use the following questions to reflect on how you care for yourself—physically and emotionally—and what it means to support both your resilience and your need for rest at this stage of life.

> *What messages from my body have gone unnoticed until now?*

⟋⟍ *How do I honor my need for both resilience and rest?*

⟋⟍ *What does wholeness mean to me at this stage of life?*

TEN

Sacred Solitude

*"Nowhere can man find a quieter or more
untroubled
retreat than in his own soul."*

MARCUS AURELIUS

We don't talk enough about the ache of loneliness. It still carries a kind of shame, as if to admit it is to confess some personal failing—as though being alone, or even just feeling as if we're alone, is something we should have figured out how to solve by now. The truth is that loneliness visits all of us, and solitude is something most of us enjoy and benefit from on occasion.

LONELINESS VS. ALONENESS

Loneliness doesn't discriminate by relationship status or personality type. It can show up in the silence after a partner has died, in a marriage that no longer feels alive, or within the interactions of a group of people where we feel unseen. What matters isn't whether loneliness arrives—as it will for every woman at some point in her life—what matters is how we meet it.

This chapter is about reframing solitude not as lack, but as sacred. About learning to hold ourselves when the silence gets heavy. About understanding that being alone is not a measure of our worth, but a mirror: It shows us what in us still needs tending, loving, softening.

There's a critical distinction between loneliness and aloneness. Loneliness is an ache—a felt sense of disconnection. It signals longing, not weakness. Aloneness, on the other hand, can be deeply restorative. It is the space in which we hear ourselves most clearly. It is solitude, not isolation.

Our culture does a poor job of teaching us how to be comfortable being alone. We're taught to seek connection outside ourselves, often before we've cultivated a sense of inner companionship. But sovereign living asks us to build a home within—a place of internal safety and belonging so that we can meet loneliness with curiosity instead of fear.

When we stop running from solitude, aloneness begins to offer us benefits.

Clarity.

Spaciousness.

Even joy.

THE GRIEF OF UNSHARED SPACES

There is sometimes grief in solo living, and it deserves to be honored. This can be not just the grief of a relationship lost or naturally ended, but the grief of an imagined future that never arrived. The quiet at night can feel deafening to those of us who are accustomed to being surrounded by a family. The absence of someone special with whom to share the mundane—a morning coffee, a bad joke, a small win—can feel like its own kind of loss.

Especially after a divorce or a partner dies, it's common to grieve the rituals we no longer perform, such as setting a table for two, sharing the day's stories, reaching for another body in the dark. We grieve the mirrored life—how it reflected us back to ourselves. And often, we grieve the selves we were in connection: Perhaps we perceived ourselves to be softer, funnier, braver, more generous. Solo living asks us to locate those parts within and learn to animate them again—this time not in reaction to another's presence and feedback, but in devotion to ourselves.

There can be grief after a breakup in admitting we deliberately chose the solo path. That it was not forced upon us by the choice to divorce, as if it were widowhood, but was born of discernment. That our feelings of liberation are sometimes shadowed by sorrow can feel confusing. But happiness, sadness, relief, and uncertainty can coexist in us. All kinds of emotional responses are honest in these scenarios.

Recognition of grief is recognition of a truth, and accepting this truth can be healing. When we allow ourselves to feel the full emotional spectrum of solo living—the ache, the beauty, the freedom—we begin to move forward with integrity through our lives rather than avoidance of our solitude. We begin to trust that we can hold ourselves. Eventually we have full faith and confidence in our sovereignty. We live courageously, doing as we please all day long, and recognize we always had more strength than we perhaps admitted.

We understand that we can be with ourselves fully—without needing to numb, flee, or perform. That we can meet our own ache with compassion, our own joy with presence. That we are capable of offering ourselves the steadiness we once sought from others. That we don't need anyone else's permission to do whatever we feel like doing. We just need our own. At last.

This final recognition takes the residual sting out of grief.

SOLO LIVING AS SOVEREIGN GROUND

There is something wildly liberating about waking up in a life that belongs only to you. About not making yourself smaller for someone else's comfort. About eating when you're hungry, sleeping when you're tired, and deciding, each day, what your presence will serve.

Solo living can be more than a circumstance; it can be a practice. A declaration. A sacred ground upon which a woman claims her authority.

To live alone is not to live unloved. It is to create a life curated entirely by you, for you. You can exercise the power of choosing your own rhythms, your own aesthetics, your own daily rituals. There is remarkable freedom, and deliciousness, in waking up and asking *What do I need today?* and then answering without negotiation.

Sovereign solitude is not necessarily about isolation. It's about integration. About being with other people when you want, and not being with them when you don't want. Solitude allows you to feel your life from the inside out. It gives you the spaciousness to notice what nourishes or depletes you, to sense when you're acting from self-trust versus self-protection.

In the absence of constant external feedback, your inner voice grows clearer—and bolder. Which is why even those of us who still have romantic partners and children residing in our homes can benefit from taking a solo retreat periodically.

Extended solitude reveals to us a calmer kind of strength we possess—the kind not forged in performance, but in presence. For when you're alone you become the one who witnesses your own evolution. The one who shows up every day without fanfare, who makes the bed or leaves it messy, tends the meal, and speaks the truth aloud even when no one else hears it.

This strength is not loud, but it is unwavering. It is dignity lived daily.

This is the sovereign life: not free from longing, but free from self-abandonment. Not dependent on witnesses, but lit from within.

As a sovereign woman in her sixties, you are not waiting to be chosen.

You are choosing.

You are not half of a whole.

You are a world unto yourself.

Solo living at your age does not have to represent a holding pattern. It is not what happens while you're waiting for the "real" thing—a relationship, a partner, a future that's more socially legible. It can be its own whole chapter in the book of a woman's life. It's not a pause between identities. It's a place where deep clarity, autonomy, and richness can unfold. It can be a beautiful, legitimate lifestyle.

If solo living is your normal way of life, thank you for offering a great example for the rest of us in how to live as independent humans. I apologize if I ever made you feel like less of a person than those of us who made a different choice than yours. Please do not hold back on our account. Go as far as you can in being courageously yourself. We will follow as we are able.

If you are newly divorced or widowed, this experience will return you to yourself in ways no relationship ever could. If you allow. Let your solitude be sacred. Let it be sovereign. Let it be enough.

REFLECTION AND INTEGRATION

A journal invitation for your most sovereign self

Reflect on the following questions to clarify how you experience solitude and loneliness. Consider what your current needs are and how you can meet them with greater honesty and self-compassion.

_9 *What have I made loneliness mean about me? Is it true?*

_9 *When have I felt most at peace in my own company?*

_9 *What kind of solitude feels nourishing?*

_9 *What kind of solitude feels hollow?*

ELEVEN

The Myth of Reinvention

"People look for retreats for themselves—
the country, the seaside, the mountains.
But none of this is necessary. There is nowhere
that a person can find a more peaceful and
trouble-free retreat than in their own mind."

MARCUS AURELIUS

We live in an era that glorifies the pivot.

THE CULT OF REINVENTION

In our society, it is often said "If you're not changing, you're stagnating" and "If you're not transforming, you're falling behind." Reinvention has become the gospel of modern womanhood—a glamorous seduction disguised as self-empowerment. Entire industries are built on the idea that the woman you are now isn't quite enough, but if you're willing to shed your skin one more time, buy one more program, post one more heavily doctored image of yourself on a social app, well then, maybe you'll be worthy of attention. Of admiration. Of belonging. Of free gifts from corporate sponsors.

Thus, we reinvent. We downplay our years and reframe our stories. We soften our edges, rebrand our bodies, reimagine our desires. And sometimes this feels liberating. But sometimes—especially for women in their sixties and beyond—it's exhausting. Not because change is unwelcome, but because we wisely know that change as performance is unsustainable. Also because constantly becoming someone else can feel like a slow betrayal of the woman we've worked so hard to become.

Furthermore, it's tiresome because we already have plans for where to invest our life force and these superficial objectives don't measure up to them.

Reinvention, when externally motivated, begins to resemble erasure. Any time you feel as if the "before" version of you is no longer being celebrated, only tolerated, it's a sign that someone has their head up their butt. Let it not be you.

That being said, this isn't a critique of growth or change. It's a reminder that when reinvention is driven by fear of fading, rather than a desire to deepen, it becomes self-abandonment in disguise.

Whether you're in media, medicine, or motherhood, the best question isn't *How can I stay appealing?* it's *How can I stay aligned?*

The push to pivot—motivated by a desire to stay culturally palatable, to remain visible, to appear vital— comes not from sovereignty, but from grasping for survival. The question at such times becomes *Who am I trying to impress? And am I sacrificing anything in the process?*

You are not here to become someone new. You are here to become more fully yourself.

What would you do if you didn't need to change who you are to stay relevant and have a meaningful life? How would you feel if you understood that your goal at this stage of life wasn't to reinvent yourself, but to claim your full essence?

WHY REINVENTION OFTEN FEELS LIKE DISAPPEARANCE

No one warns anyone that reinvention can cause grief. We're sold the idea that shedding our old selves will feel exhilarating, like a spiritual decluttering. And sometimes it does. But often, the more profound our life transitions are—be they due to a divorce, retirement, menopause, a loss, or a new beginning— the more unmoored we feel.

Reinvention doesn't always come with a sense of freedom. Sometimes it comes with a subtle dread.

Then we ask: *Who am I without the story I've always told about myself?* That story—of being the caretaker, the partner, the professional, the fixer, the one everyone counts on—can have scaffolded our identity for decades.

Letting go of the version of yourself you most closely identify with can be frightening. Sometimes it feels like losing your reflection. The mirror changes, and suddenly, you're not sure where you went.

This is the disorientation of the in-between. You've outgrown who you were, but you haven't yet landed in being who you're becoming. The world applauds our reinventions once they're polished and presentable, but it rarely honors us when we're in the raw middle and undergoing the vulnerable unraveling.

In that raw, transitional space, many women feel invisible. Not just to others, but to themselves.

Even so, invisibility can be an invitation.

It can be the quiet where truth becomes audible.

It can be the darkroom where wholeness develops.

It is not an ending. It's a passage.

REFINEMENT OVER REINVENTION

I reiterate my earlier conjecture. What if instead of trying to become someone new, you became more yourself? I find this idea much more peaceful. It relaxes me.

Refinement is different from reinvention. It doesn't ask us to start over. It asks us to become more exact.

To sand away what no longer fits and sharpen the shape of our essence.

Reinvention is often about optics.

Refinement is about alignment. In our sixties and beyond, the need to prove ourselves starts to fade. And what's left is the gold of discernment. We no longer have to crowd our lives with striving. Refinement trusts that the women we've become have value—not because they have evolved into impressive people, but because they have stopped contorting themselves to be acceptable.

Refinement is the work of maturity. It's not loud. It's not showy. It's a sacred subtraction—the removal of what is no longer essential so the true shape of our sovereignty can emerge.

You are not here to erase your story. You are here to deepen your relationship to it.

INTEGRATION IS THE NEW BECOMING

We've been taught to keep striving for some future version of ourselves—to be the "woman who finally gets it right." But wholeness doesn't come from improvement. It comes from integration.

Integration is the practice of welcoming all parts of you—even those that feel unfinished, inconvenient, or unflattering—back into the circle. This requires you to hold space for the woman you were at thirty, at fifty, and at sixty-five, without apologizing for any of them.

You don't need to upgrade. You need to include.

This is the hidden truth: Every version of you has brought you here. The resilient one. The uncertain one. The one who stayed too long. The one who left too soon. The one who loved bravely and lost badly. Every version had a role. Every version had a reason.

Integration says: "Thank you. I'll take it from here."

HOW TO RECOGNIZE WHEN YOU'RE ALREADY HOME

One of the biggest myths of reinvention is that clarity comes with drama. That a big life demands a big change. But the most profound transformations are often so quiet that they feel like nothing at all. One day, you just stop trying to be anyone else. You speak more slowly. You choose more selectively. You show up less often, but more fully.

This is what it feels like to come home to yourself. There's no parade. No big reveal. Just a subtle internal click that says, *Ah. Here I am.*

You'll recognize you've come home when you:

- No longer explain.

- Stop asking people what they think of your intuition.

- Feel at peace without needing to prove anything.

- Are more interested in resonance than approval.

⤴ Know the difference between discomfort
and misalignment.

Coming home to your essence is not an arrival but
an ongoing practice. A way of orienting to yourself with
reverence for your personal truth instead of critique. It's
knowing you've earned your own trust—not by
becoming perfect, but by becoming honest.
You are not a project.
You are a presence.
You are not meant to disappear into someone else's
narrative.
You are meant to dwell fully in your own.

THE SOVEREIGN WOMAN DOES NOT REINVENT, SHE REMEMBERS

There's nothing wrong with change. Life demands it.
But not all of the change we initiate is driven by a desire
for sovereignty. When change processes are
motivated by the need for survival, they can be
strategic.

Those who would sell us reinvention often say: "You
must become someone new to be seen, to be safe, to
be successful." But the sovereign woman has no
interest in proving her worthiness to live as she pleases
or discerns necessary. She takes responsibility for
keeping herself safe—thank you very much.

Long before anyone handed this woman the
language of boundaries or sovereignty, she was

already reading rooms, sensing threats, and learning how to move through a world that didn't always protect her. That, too, is power. She knows where to go to get karate lessons or study krav maga.

She is not polishing herself for consumption.

She is not branding herself for relevance.

She is not auditioning for belonging.

She is listening inward.

She is choosing consciously.

She is moving in rhythm with her own truth.

The myth of reinvention dissolves the moment we stop running from ourselves and start standing in our depth. You do not need to reinvent. You need to return.

Return to what you once knew, but forgot.

Return to what was always yours, but never claimed.

Return to the woman who was never missing, only muted.

The work of the sovereign self is not to rise from the ashes, but to walk—as a whole, wise, and fully awake being—through the fire and into the light.

REFLECTION AND INTEGRATION

A journal invitation for your sovereign self

Use the following questions to reflect on how you've shaped your identity over time. Consider where deeper integration and refinement—rather than reinvention— might now serve your growth and authenticity.

〇 *Is there somewhere that I confused reinvention with escape?*

〇 *What parts of myself have I prematurely discarded in order to be "new"?*

〇 *What would it look like to refine who I am, rather than redesign myself?*

〇 *What truths have followed me across every version of my life?*

〇 *How will I know when I've come home to myself?*

TWELVE

Embodiment of Emotional Sovereignty

*"Waste no more time arguing about what
a good man should be. Be one."*

MARCUS AURELIUS

B y the time we reach our sixties, the work of fully embodying our essence is no longer theoretical. We are not striving to become someone, but to be who we already are without pretense or self-sabotage. This is the stage of life when our emotional mastery becomes visible in how we move through the world: not as a performance, but as an unmistakable presence.

LIVING FROM THE INSIDE OUT

As a sovereign woman, you do not shape-shift to make others comfortable.

You do not lead with apology or soften your power with disclaimers.

You do not abandon your truth, your needs, or your values in the name of being understood.

You don't contort yourself to make others comfortable.

You speak not to be approved of, but to be honest.

You live from the inside out.

Your values are operational, not aspirational.

Your boundaries are lived, not explained.

Your clarity is not forced, it flows.

Self-embodiment is not loud because it doesn't need to be. Others can feel your calm, grounded energy when you enter a room. They pick up on the discernment in your gaze, and perceive your integrity in your silence.

To live from the inside out is to let your interior—your intuition, your wisdom, your knowing you. It is to move at your own pace. To speak only when it matters. To rest when your body calls. To act only from alignment, never from obligation.

This is emotional sovereignty—not as a concept, but as a way of being. If you are just turning sixty, rest assured that it is something you will no longer aspire to. It will be something you inhabit.

OWNING PRESENCE, DEPTH, AND SELF-DIRECTION

A woman in her sixties who has done her inner work radiates something that cannot be faked: *presence.* Not performative, not attention-seeking, not reliant on external validation, her impactful presence is the natural byproduct of her depth of being.

By this age, you have lived long enough to see behind the curtain of most illusions about success, beauty, relationships, and other sources of self-worth. So now, you don't feel compelled to prove anything. You simply *are*. And that is more than enough.

Owning your presence means understanding that your energy is your authority. That you do not need to dominate a room to affect it. You do not need to be the loudest voice to be heard.

You do not need to be visible on everyone else's terms to be fully seen by yourself.

Depth becomes your rhythm.

You are no longer interested in surface-level connection, conversations that skim, or performances that exhaust. You crave honesty, nuance, mutuality—and if that is not available, you are equally at peace in solitude.

Self-direction becomes your second nature.

You no longer ask for permission.

You no longer overexplain.

You no longer seek consensus to validate your choices.

You are not unkind. You are not inflexible. You are simply *clear*. And that clarity is the result of decades of living, observing, feeling, and refining.

If you're like me and the other sixty-something-year-old women I know, then you no longer outsource your decisions to trends, expectations, or fears. You have reached a stage of life when you are guided by something more enduring: your own truth.

Being inwardly directed is not indicative of detachment. It is an expression of your devotion to what is real, to what is yours, to what is now.

A SOVEREIGN LIFE: REFINED, UNSHAKEN, AND UNAPOLOGETICALLY YOURS

Everything you have done and learned and experienced converges once you reach your sixties: not in a grand finale, but in the clarity of your own becoming. By now, emotional mastery is no longer something you must reach for; it is something you embody. Emotional sovereignty is not a concept to you; it's just your way of being.

By now, you have refined your relationships, your inner dialogue, your presence. You have released what no longer belongs to you and redefined your definition of what it means to be alive. And in doing so, you have stepped into a different kind of power.

Not the power of dominance or force. Not the power of recognition or control. But the power of knowing who you are, and living in full alignment with that truth.

You are unshaken—not because you are unaffected, but because you are rooted.

You are unapologetic—not because you are hard, but because you are honest.

THE SOVEREIGN SELF

You are sovereign—not because you stand alone, but because you stand fully in yourself.

This is what a sovereign life looks like:

- Choosing how you spend your time, and with whom.
- Moving through the world on your terms, at your pace.
- Making decisions from clarity, not fear.
- Living from the inside out, moment by moment, breath by breath.

Ultimately, there is no arrival to emotional sovereignty. There is only deepening.

Each day becomes a new opportunity to live more honestly, more elegantly, more freely. You are no longer striving to be someone—you are simply being, and that is the most powerful act of all.

You are not behind.

You are not in decline.

You are not done.

You are becoming—still.

And it is breathtaking to witness.

REFLECTION AND INTEGRATION

A journal invitation for your sovereign self

Reflect on how you're embodying emotional sovereignty now and how you intend to carry it forward. Let the following questions help you name the qualities, commitments, and presence you wish to strengthen and personify in this next chapter of your life.

- *What does emotional sovereignty feel like in my body?*

- *How will I recognize the woman I am becoming?*

- *What promise am I making to myself as I move forward?*

THIRTEEN

The Spirituality of Not-Knowing

"If you want to improve, be content to be thought foolish and stupid."

EPICTETUS

At some point, the map you are following disappears. Maybe the career you built no longer excites you. Maybe the role you have been playing—as mother, partner, caregiver, planner, provider—shifts or dissolves. Maybe the identity that got you confidently through earlier decades begins to feel tight, outdated, or subtly misaligned. Now, suddenly, you've landed somewhere between being who you've been and who you're becoming, and the terrain is unfamiliar. There is no clear instruction for navigating this landscape. No ten-step guide. No vision board that would make it all make sense.

You have entered the space of not knowing. And for women in their sixties and beyond, the unknown is both

117

holy and disorienting. It's time to let go of your previous life plan.

LETTING GO OF YOUR LIFE PLAN

For most of our lives, we've been taught that not knowing is a problem to solve. A gap to fill. A weakness to correct. We've been praised for our clarity, our decisiveness, and our ability to plan, so we've learned to equate certainty with competence. We've crafted our lives as if we were drawing blueprints—describing objects with measurable, visible, achievable dimensions.

But what happens when the blueprint of life that you've been following becomes irrelevant to what you want to experience in the future?

What happens when you intuit that the most honest thing you could do for yourself right now is let go of your existing map or GPS instructions—and recalculate?

At first, there's fear. Of course there would be. Fear of aimlessness. Fear of irrelevance. Fear of what others will think. But beneath those fears lies something else—something that contradicts mental anxiety messages: relief.

Relief that you no longer have to perform with certainty.

Relief that you finally allow yourself to pause, without apology, without explanation.

Relief that you no longer have anything to prove.

Ditching the plan is not a breakdown. It is a sacred unmapping, a sign of the emergence of your conscious sovereignty.

LIVING THE QUESTIONS

In a 1903 letter to a young poet he was mentoring, Rainer Maria Rilke writes: "Be patient toward all that is unsolved in your heart and try to love the questions themselves . . ."[1] It's good advice for us all. In our earlier years, this idea would have been unthinkable. We were rewarded for our fast answers, quick decisions, confident conclusions. We were trained to control uncertainty—to manage it into submission—so we learned to rush the question in search of its answer.

But in our current season of life, the questions we're contemplating have begun to change shape. They are growing deeper, more textured. They don't want quick fixes. They want to be lived and patiently considered. They sound like:

- *What do I want now that no one else is deciding for me?*

- *What am I still carrying that's no longer mine to hold?*

- *What would my days look like if I moved at the pace of truth?*

These are not questions to solve. They are invitations to inhabit.

119

Living the questions means learning to sit in the space between clarity and ambiguity without losing yourself. It means letting silence speak before you fill it. It means learning to trust the slow unfurling of insight, rather than demanding revelations on command.

To live a question is to say: *I do not need to know yet, and I trust that knowing will come. Not as lightning, but as light—slowly, gently, in its own time.*

RELEASING THE PERFORMANCE OF CONTROL

Certainty can be faked.

Many of us have mastered the art of pretending to know. We do performances to show we know how to keep things together, how to reassure others, how to move forward even when the ground beneath us is shaking. We've done them for decades—at work, in our relationships, within our families. And as a result, we've been praised for our competence, for our steadiness, for our ability to make sense of the chaos.

In our sixties, our performances start to feel heavy. Hollow. And if we're being honest, unnecessary.

There is liberation in admitting: *I don't know.*

Not as a confession, but as a spiritual stance.

Not from collapse, but from clarity.

When we stop performing control, we stop contorting ourselves to match other people's expectations. We stop narrating our lives in a way that makes others comfortable. We begin to let the truth of our not-knowing soften us. Expand us. Control is not the same as clarity, and certainty is not the same as wisdom. These days we want the real things, not their pale substitutes.

To live without a script is to begin listening finally for the deeper rhythm of our own spirit. The one that isn't imposed. The one that rises from within.

BECOMING A CHANNEL, NOT A CHOREOGRAPHER

In our striving years, we acted as if we were choreo-graphers. We managed the outcomes, moved the pieces, took responsibility for everyone's experience. We scheduled. We anticipated. We shaped and reshaped our lives to make things happen.

But now, we are being invited to do something different. Now, we are being invited to become channels.

A channel doesn't orchestrate.

A channel opens.

A channel listens.

A channel receives.

Becoming channels doesn't mean we will stop participating in our lives. It means we will learn to allow them to unfold from a deeper source. It means we will stop micromanaging our evolution and start trusting that life has intelligence, too.

We don't need to force clarity, only to prepare the ground for it to arrive.

This is what it means to become a channel.

⟡ To align with integrity

⟡ To stay present to your body

⟡ To listen without grasping

⟡ To trust the timing of what is ready to emerge

As a channel, you will find that your role is no longer to direct. Your role is to stay open—to move from resonance, rather than out of reaction.

TRUSTING THE WISDOM OF THE UNKNOWN

A remembering happens in this season of life as you begin to see all the times you didn't know, and yet were guided. The relationship that ended and left you stronger. The job you didn't get that made space for something better. The silence that led to clarity. The loss that taught you how to live. Subtle guidance was involved.

As you remember slowly, you will begin to trust the unknown. Not as a void, but as a field. Not as emptiness, but as potential. Not as confusion, but as sacred unfolding.

The wisdom of not knowing is that it returns you to the present. It keeps you from outsourcing your authority to certainty. It allows you to release your grip on the future and come back to what is real, right here, right now.

And from this place, you can still build. You can still create.

But now it comes from listening. Not proving.

This is a different kind of self-leadership—one rooted inward, not performed outward.

It's not about projecting strength or control; it's about inhabiting your truth from the inside out.

It's not linear, but intuitive.

Not scripted, but sovereign.

THE PRESENCE BEYOND THE PLAN

In your sixties and beyond, there is a grace that emerges when you stop narrating your life as a series of goals and start inhabiting it as a series of moments.

You begin to notice the space between things.

You begin to honor the pause.

You begin to let uncertainty be a teacher, not a threat.

Not knowing is neither a flaw, nor a failure. It is a sign that you are still becoming. And becoming never needs to be explained. Only lived.

This is the spirituality of not knowing:

_⚭ A return to presence.

_ᴐ A loosening of the grip.

_ᴐ A homecoming to what cannot be planned, but only trusted.

The sovereign path is not mapped, but felt. Not certain, but sacred. Not figured out, but fully alive.

REFLECTION AND INTEGRATION

A journal invitation for your sovereign self

Use the following questions to examine where you may be holding on too tightly—and where greater ease, trust, or patience could support you now. Let this reflection open space for more clarity and flow.

_ᴐ *Where in my life am I still gripping for control, and what would it feel like to loosen my grip?*

_ᴐ *What questions have I been trying to answer too quickly?*

_ᴐ *Where has not knowing led me to deeper truth in the past?*

_ᴐ *What would it mean to live without a plan, but with presence?*

_ᴐ *What part of me is ready to rest in the wisdom of uncertainty?*

CONCLUSION

Live on Your Own Terms

"While it is in your power, be good."

MARCUS AURELIUS

We live in a culture that views aging through the lens of diminishment. As though the further we move from youth, the further we drift from value, relevance, vitality. But what if we turned that story inside out? What if aging—especially for women—was not a slow erasure, but a kind of ascension?

What if the sixties were not a soft landing, but a rising?

Because that is what this journey truly is: a return to center, a refinement of identity, a deepening of presence. This is the decade where we come home to ourselves. Not the selves we've shaped due to expectation, but the selves shaped by wisdom. Not the selves curated for the sake of others, but the ones we ourselves have cultivated through clarity, truth-telling, and sovereign choice.

125

I see you. You have learned to feel without flinching.
To speak without apology.
To love without abandoning yourself.
To let go without collapsing.
To stand still without shrinking.
This is not decline.
This is ascension.
You are no longer a product—no longer what the world made you.
You are the author of what comes next.
You are sovereign.
You are whole.
Yes, you are still becoming, but perhaps the first time, you are doing it entirely on your own terms.

THE SOVEREIGN SELF TOOLKIT

The Sovereign Self Toolkit is a collection of evidence-informed practices that support emotional regulation, self-inquiry, and embodied aging. Use what resonates.

DAILY RITUALS FOR DEVELOPING EMOTIONAL MASTERY

These simple rituals are designed to bring you back to your center—not to fix, but to feel.

- Three-Breath Reset. Wherever you are, close your eyes and take three slow, conscious breaths. Let the exhale be longer than the inhale. This pattern recalibrates the nervous system.

- Name It to Hold It. Each morning and/or evening, name the dominant emotion in your body without judging or analyzing it. Let it be seen.

- Five-Minute Stillness. Sit in silence with no agenda. Let yourself feel what's underneath the noise. You do not need to be productive here. You only need to be present.

JOURNALING PROMPTS FOR SOVEREIGNTY

Return to these prompts when you feel untethered or unclear. Open a fresh page in your journal and write in a stream of consciousness about one or all of them for as long as you like.

- What am I no longer available for?
- What part of me is asking to be witnessed today?
- What do I know now that I used to doubt?
- What would feel most nourishing to me in this moment?

EMBODIMENT RITUALS

The body carries wisdom that the mind forgets. These simple rituals are invitations to come home to your body.

- **Walk Barefoot (Even Briefly).** Place your feet on grass, wood, or sand. Let the energy of the earth recalibrate you.
- **Stretch.** Move intuitively. Let your body lead for five minutes.
- **Put One Hand on Your Heart.** With a hand on your heart and a hand on your belly, ask, *What truth am I holding here?*

128

QUESTIONS TO RETURN TO AGAIN AND AGAIN

These are not meant to be answered once. They are lifelong companions.

_ৎ) *Who am I becoming when no one is watching?*

_ৎ) *What do I trust more now than I ever have?*

_ৎ) *How do I define power, now that I am aware it belongs to me?*

ACKNOWLEDGMENTS

My deepest appreciation extends to my beloved family—Tae, Mia, and Joe—for the grounding, love, and support they bring to my life. They are my world. With profound love and gratitude, I would like to take this opportunity to thank two remarkable women— my sister Susan Dutton Callahan and dear friend Jodi Kipperman Drutman—whose unwavering presence and unconditional love have been a constant source of strength for me.

I am grateful to my sister Cindy for her love and the family ties that continue to connect our lives. I am also grateful to my niece Alexa Serpa and her beautiful family for the love and boundless joy they so generously give—a gift beyond what words can convey.

I am grateful to Abby Tyson Ciambrone, my friend of nearly half a century, for an enduring and loving friendship I will always cherish. To Thea Samuels, I express my love and appreciation for the literal nonstop laughs we share and a friendship that is nothing short of extraordinary.

Very special thanks and love as well to Winston Simone for his steady support and encouragement, and to Joe Brauner for the same generosity and our decades-long friendship.

Finally, I offer heartfelt gratitude to my brilliant editor, Stephanie Gunning, whose insight, guidance, and care have been invaluable in shaping this book and bringing its vision to life.

And, of course, I am thankful for my faithful lap-warmer, Chili, proof that life is always better with a dog by one's side.

RECOMMENDED READING

The following books form a living library for cultivating wisdom, presence, and inner authority.

THE STOICS: FOUNDATIONS OF EMOTIONAL MASTERY

The Daily Stoic: 366 Meditations on Wisdom, Perseverance, and the Art of Living by Ryan Holiday and Stephen Hanselman (2016)

Discourses and Selected Writings by Epictetus (circa 108 CE)

How to Be a Stoic: Using Ancient Philosophy to Live a Modern Life by Massimo Pigliucci (2017)

Letters from a Stoic by Seneca (circa 65 CE)

Meditations by Marcus Aurelius (circa 161–180 CE)

PHILOSOPHY: LIVING WITH DEPTH, CLARITY, AND MORAL IMAGINATION

The Art of Living: The Classical Manual on Virtue, Happiness, and Effectiveness by Epictetus, as interpreted by Sharon Lebell (2007)

Being and Time by Martin Heidegger (1927)

The Consolations of Philosophy by Alain de Botton (2001)

The Courage to Be by Paul Tillich (1952)

The Examined Life: How We Lose and Find Ourselves by Stephen Grosz (2014)

The Great Work of Your Life: A Guide for the Journey to Your True Calling by Stephen Cope 2012)

Man's Search for Meaning by Viktor E. Frankl (1946)

On the Shortness of Life by Seneca (circa 49 CE)

The Second Mountain: The Quest for a Moral Life by David Brooks (2020)

AGING WITH DEPTH AND GRACE

Elderhood: Redefining Aging, Transforming Medicine, Reimagining Life by Louise Aronson (2019)

The Gift of Years: Growing Older Gracefully by Joan Chittister (2010)

The Inner Work of Age: Shifting from Role to Soul by Connie Zweig (2021)

This Chair Rocks: A Manifesto Against Ageism by Ashton Applewhite (2019)

Women Rowing North: Navigating Life's Currents and Flourishing as We Age by Mary Pipher (2019)

THE SOVEREIGN SELF

MEMOIR AND STORY AS MEDICINE

Braiding Sweetgrass: Indigenous Wisdom, Scientific Knowledge and The Teachings of Plants by Robin Wall Kimmerer (2013)

The Choice: Embrace the Possible by Dr. Edith Eva Eger (2017)

In the Body of the World: A Memoir of Cancer and Connection by Eve Ensler (2013)

Wave: A Memoir by Sonali Deraniyagala (2013)

When the Heart Waits: Spiritual Direction for Life's Sacred Questions by Sue Monk Kidd (1990)

EMOTIONAL AND SPIRITUAL SOVEREIGNTY

Anatomy of the Spirit: The Seven Stages of Power and Healing by Caroline Myss (1996)

The Places That Scare You: A Guide to Fearlessness in Difficult Times by Pema Chödrön (2005) *Radical Acceptance: Embracing Your Life with the Heart of Buddha* by Tara Brach (2003)

The Untethered Soul: The Journey Beyond Yourself by Michael A. Singer (2013)

Women Who Run With the Wolves: Myths and Stories of the Wild Woman Archetype by Clarissa Pinkola Estés (1992)

PLEASURE, EMBODIMENT, AND PRESENCE

Belonging: Remembering Ourselves Home by Toko-pa Turner (2017)

Come As You Are: The Surprising New Science That Will Transform Your Sex Life by Emily Nagoski (2015)

Cured: Strengthen Your Immune System and Heal Your Life by Jeffrey Rediger, M.D. (2021)

The Power of Now: A Guide to Spiritual Enlightenment by Eckhart Tolle (2004)

Sacred Woman: A Guide to Healing the Feminine Body, Mind, and Spirit by Queen Afua (2001)

WOMEN'S HEALTH AND MEDICAL TRUTH-TELLING

All in Her Head: The Truth and Lies Early Medicine Taught Us About Women's Bodies and Why

It Matters Today by Elizabeth Comen, M.D. (2024)

Doing Harm: The Truth About How Bad Medicine and Lazy Science Leave Women Dismissed,

The Female Body Bible: Make Your Body Work for You by Emma Ross, Ph.D., Bella Smith,

M.D., and Baz Moffat (2024)

Misdiagnosed, and Sick by Maya Dusenbery (2019)

Unwell Women: Misdiagnosis and Myth in a Man-Made World by Elinor Cleghorn (2021)

The Wisdom of Menopause: Creating Physical and Emotional Health During the Change, fourth edition by Christiane Northrup, M.D. (2024)

NOTES

Chapter 1: The Architecture of Emotional Mastery

Epigraph. Marcus Aurelius. *Meditations,* translated by Gregory Hays (New York: Modern Library, 2022): p. 43.

Chapter 2: The Evolution of Identity

Epigraph. Seneca. *Letters from a Stoic,* translated by Robin Campbell (London, U.K.: Penguin Books, 1969): p. 70.

Chapter 3: Time as an Ally, not an Adversary

Epigraph. Marcus Aurelius. *Meditations,* translated by Gregory Hays (New York: Modern Library, 2022): p. 167.

Chapter 4: Relationships in the Third Act

Epigraph. Seneca. *Letters from a Stoic,* translated by Robin Campbell (London, U.K.: Penguin Books, 1969): p. 54.

Chapter 5 : The Art of Emotional Curation

Epigraph. Seneca. *Letters from a Stoic,* translated by Robin Campbell (London, U.K.: Penguin Books, 1969): p. 49.

Chapter 6: The Liberation of Joy

Epigraph. Marcus Aurelius. *Meditations,* translated by Gregory Hays (New York: Modern Library, 2022): p. 111.

Chapter 7: The Practice of Stillness

Epigraph. Seneca. *Letters from a Stoic,* translated by Robin Campbell (London, U.K.: Penguin Books, 1969): p. 52.

Chapter 8: The Power of Emotional Inquiry

Epigraph. Seneca. Popular attribution: No exact source in extant works.

Chapter 9: Tending the Body, Honoring the Self

Epigraph. Eric Jorgenson. *The Almanack of Naval Ravikant: A Guide to Wealth and Happiness* (Miami, FL.: Magrathea Publishing, 2020): p. 106.

Chapter 10: Sacred Solitude

Epigraph. Marcus Aurelius. *Meditations,* translated by Gregory Hays (New York: Modern Library, 2022): p. 43.

Chapter 11: The Myth of Reinvention

Epigraph. Marcus Aurelius. *Meditations,* translated by Gregory Hays (New York: Modern Library, 2022): p. 43.

Chapter 12: Embodiment of Emotional Sovereignty

Epigraph. Marcus Aurelius. *Meditations*, translated by Gregory Hays (New York: Modern Library, 2022): p. 157.

Chapter 13: The Spirituality of Not Knowing

Epigraph. Epictetus. *Discourses and Selected Writings*, translated and edited by Robert Dobbins (London, U.K.: Penguin Books, 2008): p. 287.

1. Rainer Maria Rilke. *Letters to a Young Poet*, translated by M.D. Herter Norton (1934): p. 71.

Conclusion

Epigraph. Marcus Aurelius. *Meditations*, translated by Gregory Hays (New York: Modern Library, 2002): p. 48.

ABOUT THE AUTHOR

STACEY DUTTON is a writer, producer, and former entertainment executive whose three-decade-plus career has spanned the music, television, and creative strategy worlds. Known for her intuitive eye and voice-centered storytelling, she has guided the careers of artists, hosted and produced network television, and developed programming. *The Sovereign Self* marks her debut as an author—and a return to her own deepest truths.

Visit Stacey's website LiveSovereignSelf.com

www.ingramcontent.com/pod-product-compliance
Lightning Source LLC
Chambersburg PA
CBHW060429130626
46555CB00005B/2278